G000098351

Hello lovely readers, and welcome to our brand new Yearbook! Every year we package together a special collection of dishes from the past 12 months of Jamie magazine - it's like a big, beautiful highlights reel of what we've been up to, which is a great way to celebrate all the gorgeous things we've been cooking up. It's all here, and divvied up into handy sections so you can easily find what you're looking for. You'll find a nice mix of short, no-fuss recipes and great big showstoppers for when you feel like pushing the boat out - think seriously good salads and outrageously delicious meaty feasts, as well as nutritious grains, super-comforting soups and lots of sweet treats, too. We've also got a whole chapter dedicated to drinks, and there's an extra section jam-packed with all those useful bits and bobs, such as chutneys, dips and sauces. Think of this Yearbook as your menu-planning sidekick, if you like. I hope you'll find plenty here to inspire you for the next year and beyond. Happy cooking, guys!

Picking the recipes for our annual Yearbook is always an exciting time at *Jamie*, not least because it's when we get to debate which ones to give you. Some of my favourites, like slow-cooked tomato and merguez spaghetti (p32), espeto de sardines (p82) and gado-gado (p59) even made it in! There's something really satisfying to see the fruits of so many amazing issues come together, and also gives us the chance to introduce our lovely mag to a new audience of people who love to cook as much as we do. To readers old and new alike, we wish you a fantastic year in food!

Into social media?
Us too! Let's be friends

Editor at Large

Editor

ALL RECIPES TESTED IN THE JAMIE OLIVER KITCHENS

CONTENTS

50

116

169

start your day the **happy** egg way

At the happy egg co. our hens aren't just any hens - they're our girls. And we're passionate about doing everything we can to keep our girls happy. We give them lots of space to roam, sand pits for dust bathing and shady trees to cool off under, because of one simple belief: happy hens lay really tasty eggs.

For delicious recipes and eggy inspiration visit **thehappyegg.co.uk**

BREAKFASTS & BRUNCHES

SWEET POTATO & PECAN BREAD

This loaf is wonderfully moist and naturally sweet. Serve warm from the oven, or toasted, and spread with the pecan butter.

Makes 2 loaves, each serves 8 Ⓥ

- 250ml olive oil, plus 2 tbsp, plus extra for greasing
- 1kg sweet potatoes, peeled and cut into 2-3cm chunks
- 2 tsp ground cinnamon
- Finely grated zest of 2 oranges, juice of 1
- 150g pecans
- 4 large eggs
- 100g plain yoghurt
- 2 tsp mixed spice
- 400g plain flour
- 4 tsp bicarbonate of soda

Pecan butter
- 400g pecans
- 75ml coconut oil
- 2 tsp vanilla extract

ULTIMATE BREAKFAST SHAKE

1 Preheat the oven to 170C/gas 3. Grease and line two 1-litre loaf tins. Pop the sweet potato in a roasting tray. Sprinkle over the cinnamon and a good pinch of sea salt, then drizzle with the 2 tablespoons of olive oil.
2 Pour the orange juice into the tray. Toss everything together and roast for 35-40 minutes, until golden and cooked through. Set aside to cool.
3 Put 100g of the pecans in a food processor and blitz to a powder, then spoon into a bowl. Put the cooled, cooked sweet potato in the food processor and blitz to a smooth purée. Add the eggs, yoghurt, mixed spice, orange zest, ground pecans and olive oil, then blitz again until everything is well combined.
4 Add the flour and bicarb of soda and pulse until just combined (don't overwork it), then divide between the loaf tins. Chop the remaining 50g of pecans and sprinkle over the top, then bake for about 1 hour, until golden and cooked through. Leave to cool completely before serving.
5 To make the butter, scatter the pecans on a baking sheet and pop into the oven, still at 170C/gas 3, for 12-15 minutes or until golden and toasted. Leave to cool, then blitz in a food processor for 8 minutes, or until you have a smooth paste. You'll need to stop it a couple of times and scrape the mixture down the bowl with a spatula.
6 Pour in the coconut oil, vanilla and a good pinch of sea salt, then blitz again. Transfer to a dish, cover and store in the fridge until needed. Serve with the sweet potato bread.

Per serving 479 cals, 35.7g fat (6.2g sat fats), 7.3g protein, 34.7g carbs, 5.6g sugars

ULTIMATE BREAKFAST SHAKE

Smoothies are a great way to fill up on enough fruit, nuts and seeds to keep you going until lunch.

Serves 2 ⒹⒻ ⒼⒻ Ⓥ ⒱Ⓖ

- 750ml tomato juice
- 500g frozen berries, plus extra to garnish
- 600ml almond milk
- 6 medjool dates, destoned
- 4 brazil nuts, chopped
- 1 tbsp freshly milled flax seed
- 1 tbsp desiccated coconut

1 Blitz all of the ingredients in a food processor or blender until you have a consistency you like. Chill in the fridge then serve cold, or pour over ice and top with extra berries.

Per serving 327 cals, 14.2g fat (3.6g sat fats), 9.6g protein, 41g carbs, 40.9g sugars

SPICED MUESLI BARS

SPICED MUESLI BARS
Makes 12 Ⓥ

- Vegetable oil, for greasing
- 3 large very ripe bananas
- 100ml milk (dairy or nut milk)
- Finely grated zest of 1 orange
- ½ tsp ground cinnamon
- 250g rolled oats
- 1 tbsp sesame seeds
- 125g medjool dates, stoned and finely chopped
- 50g pistachios, chopped

1 Preheat the oven to 180C/gas 4. Grease a 9 x 9cm square cake tin and line it with baking paper. In a large mixing bowl, mash the bananas into a purée, then mix in the milk, orange zest, cinnamon and a pinch of salt.
2 Stir in the rest of the ingredients and evenly press into the tray. Bake for 25 minutes or until lovely and golden all over. Remove from the oven, but leave it on. Allow to cool in the tin for 5 minutes. Cut in half, then cut each half into six bars.
3 Line a baking sheet with greaseproof paper and place the bars, upside-down, in a row. Pop back in the oven for 10 minutes to crisp up all over, then leave to cool. Serve immediately or store in an airtight container for up to a week.

Per serving 148 cals, 4.7g fat (0.8g sat fats), 4g protein, 21.9g carbs, 9.3g sugars

SWEDISH SMASHED HASH
Serves 6 Ⓓ Ⓕ

- 700g potatoes,
- 2 carrots, peeled
- 2 parsnips, peeled
- Olive oil
- 2 onions, peeled and finely sliced
- 4 sausages
- 2 tsp english mustard
- ½ small bunch of dill, leaves picked and chopped
- 1 small bunch of flat-leaf parsley, leaves picked and chopped
- Juice of 1 lemon
- 2 dill pickles, finely chopped (optional)
- 6 large eggs

1 Bring a large pan of salted water to the boil. Cut the potatoes, carrots and parsnips into 1cm cubes. Add the potato and carrot to the pan and cook for 10-12 minutes, until cooked through, adding the parsnip after 5 minutes. Drain all the veg in a colander and leave to steam-dry.
2 Add a good glug of olive oil to a large, non-stick frying pan and pop in the onion. Sauté over a low-medium heat for 5 minutes, until softened slightly, but not coloured.
3 Squeeze the meat out of the sausages and crumble it into the pan. Fry for a further 10-15 minutes, stirring occasionally, until the meat has browned and cooked through.
4 Add the drained veg to the pan and turn the heat up a little. Fry for about 15 minutes, occasionally giving it a stir and lightly mashing it as you go; you want a caramelised, slightly broken-down hash. Stir your mustard into the veg while cooking, to give it all a light mustard coating.
5 Meanwhile, place a medium pan of salted water on to boil, ready to cook the eggs.
6 Stir half of the herbs through the hash and place the rest in a small bowl. Add the lemon juice and stir through the pickles, if using.
7 When it's ready, season the hash and keep on a low heat while you poach the eggs. Crack the eggs into separate tea cups, pour into the boiling water and poach for 3 minutes, or until done how you like them. Remove with a slotted spoon and serve on top of the hash. Finish by scattering over the lemony herb mixture. Serve straight away.

Per serving 381 cals, 19.2g fat (5.7g sat fats), 16.5g protein, 38.4g carbs, 10.8g sugars

NUTTY OAT PANCAKES

EGGY CHILLI CRUMPETS & SMOKED BACON

BANANA & SESAME FRITTERS

Serves 4 ⓥ

- 2 ripe bananas
- 100g self-raising flour
- 2 eggs, beaten
- 1 tsp baking powder
- 2 tbsp golden caster sugar
- 4 tbsp milk
- A pinch of cinnamon or nutmeg
- 1 tbsp sesame seeds
- 1 tbsp veg oil
- Honey and yoghurt, to serve

1 Mash the bananas in a bowl, then add the flour, beaten egg, baking powder, sugar, milk, cinnamon or nutmeg and the sesame seeds. Whisk until combined.
2 Grease a large, non-stick frying pan with the veg oil and place over a high heat. Working in batches, drop large tablespoonfuls of batter into the pan and cook for 2–3 minutes, or until the base has set. Flip over and cook for 2–3 minutes, until golden. Transfer to a plate and keep warm.
3 Serve the fritters warm with a dollop of yoghurt on the side and a generous drizzle of honey.

Per serving 251 cals, 8.4g fat (1.7g sat fats), 7.3g protein, 39.3g carbs, 19.2g sugars

NUTTY OAT PANCAKES

Makes 10–12 pancakes ⓥ

- 100g porridge oats
- 200g wholemeal self-raising flour
- 150ml milk
- 200ml buttermilk
- 2 tbsp vegetable oil, plus extra for cooking
- 1 egg
- 100g chopped walnuts
- Berries, yoghurt and honey, to serve

1 In a blender, blitz the oats until fine. Tip into a bowl and mix in the flour. In another bowl, combine the milk, buttermilk, oil and egg and whisk until smooth.
2 Whisk the wet ingredients into the dry – don't overmix it – before stirring in the walnuts.
3 Place a lightly oiled non-stick frying pan over a medium heat and, in batches, dollop large spoonfuls of batter into the pan and cook for 2–3 minutes each side, until risen and lightly browned.
4 Serve the pancakes with berries, yoghurt and a drizzle of honey.

Per serving 214 cals, 11.7g fat (1.7g sat fats), 7g protein, 20.7g carbs, 2.4g sugars

EGGY CHILLI CRUMPETS & SMOKED BACON

Serves 4

- 8 rashers of smoked streaky bacon
- Olive oil
- 4 eggs
- 2 red chillies, deseeded and finely chopped
- 4 crumpets
- A small knob of butter
- Watercress, to serve

1 Heat a large frying pan over a high heat, then add the bacon and a small drizzle of oil. Cook for 5 minutes, turning halfway, or until crisp. Set the bacon aside and reduce the heat.
2 Meanwhile, in a bowl, whisk your eggs with a pinch of seasoning and most of the chilli. Soak each crumpet for 1 minute on each side. Add the butter to your bacon pan, then cook the crumpets for 2 minutes on each side, until golden and cooked.
3 Serve with the bacon rashers, watercress and scatter over the reserved chilli.

Per serving 314 cals, 18.7g fat (6.7g sat fats), 15.4g protein, 23g carbs, 1.9g sugars

KEDGEREE BREAKFAST TARTS

This is a lovely brunch dish for a special occasion – and it's also brilliant if you've got any leftover kedgeree to use up!

Makes 8

- 1kg smoked haddock
- 4 bay leaves
- 1.5 litres milk
- 160g long-grain rice
- 2 tbsp olive oil
- 1 red onion, peeled and finely chopped
- A thumb-sized piece of ginger, peeled and grated
- 1 garlic clove, peeled and finely chopped
- 2 tbsp curry powder
- 1 tbsp mustard powder
- 3 large tomatoes, grated with a box grater
- Juice and zest of 2 lemons
- 8 eggs
- 8 small sprigs of coriander, to serve

Tomato & chilli sauce

- 3 tbsp olive oil
- 1 onion, peeled and finely sliced
- 1 small red chilli, deseeded and finely chopped
- 2 garlic cloves, peeled and finely chopped
- 1 tsp dried oregano
- 2 x 250g tins chopped tomatoes
- 2 tbsp tomato paste

Pastry

- 500g plain flour
- 250g cold butter, diced
- 2 eggs, beaten

Chilli glaze

- 2 small red chillies, deseeded and finely chopped
- 3 tbsp olive oil

1 Start by making the sauce. Heat the oil in a saucepan over a medium heat and sauté the onion, chilli, garlic and oregano until softened, about 5 minutes. Season and add the tinned tomatoes, tomato paste and 200ml of water. Lower the heat and simmer, stirring occasionally, for 40 minutes, or until thickened. Transfer the sauce to a bowl until ready to use.

2 For the pastry, combine the flour and a pinch of salt in a food processor. Add the butter and blitz until it resembles breadcrumbs. Add the eggs and about 60ml of cold water to form a dough. Wrap in cling film and chill in the fridge for 20 minutes.

3 Preheat the oven to 180C/gas 4. Roll out the dough 5mm thick and cut out the pastry in circles large enough to line eight 12cm tart tins (or 14-16 x 10cm tins). Lay the pastry in the tins, pushing it down gently, then trim away any excess. Line each tin with baking paper, then fill with baking beans or uncooked rice and bake for 15-20 minutes.

4 Remove the paper and beans or rice, then return the tins to the oven and cook for a further 6-8 minutes, until the pastry is golden.

5 Meanwhile, make the kedgeree. Place the haddock and bay leaves in a large pan and cover with the milk. Bring to the boil over a medium heat, lower the temperature and simmer for 10 minutes, until cooked. Allow the fish to cool slightly, then transfer it to a bowl and flake into chunks.

6 Cook the rice in salted water for about 15 minutes, then drain and add to the bowl with the haddock.

7 Heat the olive oil in a large frying pan over a medium heat. Add the onion, ginger, garlic, curry and mustard powders and sauté for 5 minutes, or until softened. Add the grated tomatoes, season well and cook for 10-12 minutes. Preheat the oven to 200C/gas 6.

8 Add the fish, rice, lemon zest and juice to the onion mixture, stir well and cook for a few more minutes. Transfer back to the bowl and allow to cool for 5 minutes.

9 Divide the kedgeree between your tart tins, making a small well in the middle of each one. Crack an egg into every well, place the tins on a baking tray and pop in the oven for 20-25 minutes, or until the eggs are cooked to your liking.

10 Meanwhile, make the chilli glaze by combining the ingredients in a

small saucepan and cooking over a medium heat for 10 minutes.

11 Divide the kedgeree tarts between plates. Brush the top of each tart with chilli glaze, garnish with coriander and serve with the tomato and chilli sauce on the side.

Per serving 899 cals, 49.5g fat (19.8g sat fats), 43.2g protein, 74.5g carbs, 8.5g sugars

JOOLS OLIVER'S BREAKFAST ON THE GO
(Pictured on p7)

"I make this super-simple breakfast and put it in plastic tubs for the girls to eat on the way to school if we're running out the door or have an early start," says Jools.

Serves 6 ⓥ

- 1 apple, coarsely grated
- 100g dried fruit, such as blueberries, cherries, sultanas and raisins
- 200g porridge oats
- 1 heaped tbsp flaxseeds
- 500ml unsweetened almond or regular milk
- 1 large ripe banana, peeled and sliced at an angle
- 4 tbsp natural yoghurt
- A handful of mixed nuts, roughly chopped
- 2 handfuls of fresh raspberries or blueberries, or a mixture of both
- Runny honey (optional)

1 Put the apple, dried fruit, porridge oats, flaxseeds and milk in a bowl and mix well. Cover the bowl with cling film and leave in the fridge overnight to soak and swell.

2 In the morning, give it a good stir and divide between tubs or bowls. Top each serving with some sliced banana and a spoonful of yoghurt (this will help to stop the banana turning brown).

3 Sprinkle over the nuts and berries. Drizzle with a little honey, if using, then pop the lid on – and don't forget to take some spoons!

Per serving 280 cals, 8.8g fat (1.3g sat fats), 7.3g protein, 41.3g carbs, 20.9g sugars

KEDGEREE BREAKFAST TARTS

CREAMY SCRAMBLED
EGGS WITH SALMON

BUCKWHEAT
PORRIDGE

FIG SMOOTHIE

CREAMY SCRAMBLED EGGS WITH SALMON
Serves 4
- 8 eggs
- 4 tbsp half-fat crème fraîche
- 15g butter
- 200g smoked salmon, chopped
- 8 slices of sourdough bread, toasted
- 2 tbsp chopped fresh chives

1 In a bowl, beat the eggs and crème fraîche together with a little salt and freshly ground black pepper.
2 Melt the butter in a non-stick pan over a low heat and, once foaming, pour in the egg mixture. Cook gently, stirring until the egg has thickened and is almost scrambled.
3 Stir in the salmon and keep cooking until the eggs are done to your liking – the slower you cook your scrambled eggs, the creamier they become.
4 Place 2 slices of toasted bread on each plate. Top with the scrambled eggs and a sprinkling of chopped chives, and serve immediately.
Per serving 503 cals, 24.3g fat (8g sat fats), 34.4g protein, 35.8g carbs, 2.1g sugars

BUCKWHEAT PORRIDGE
Serves 2 (DF) (GF) (V)
- 400ml unsweetened almond milk
- 80g buckwheat flakes
- Honey, to taste
- 200g strawberries, halved and hulled
- 1 vanilla pod, seeds only
- Juice of ½ lemon
- 15g flaked almonds, toasted

1 Pour 300ml of the milk into a pan and add the buckwheat. Place over a medium heat and add a pinch of salt.
2 Heat the mixture, stirring, for 6 minutes, until thickened, adding adding the remaining milk towards the end to to loosen, as needed. Drizzle with honey.
3 In another pan, cook the stawberries, vanilla and lemon juice over a low heat, stirring, for 6 minutes, or until the berries have softened. Spoon the porridge into bowls and top with the stewed strawberries and the almonds.
Per serving 267 cals, 7.1g fat (0.6g sat fats), 6.7g protein, 46.6g carbs, 12.6g sugars

FIG SMOOTHIE
Serves 4 (GF) (V)
- 4 ripe figs, topped, tailed and quartered, plus extra wedges to garnish
- 1 ripe banana, peeled
- 200g greek yoghurt
- 1 tbsp honey, plus extra to drizzle
- Milk, to loosen

1 In a blender or liquidiser, blitz the figs, banana, yoghurt and honey until smooth. Add enough milk to get a desired consistency.
2 Pour into four glasses, drizzle with extra honey and garnish with the fig wedges. Serve.
Per serving 97 cals, 0.6g fat (0.3g sat fats), 6.9g protein, 17g carbs, 16.4g sugars

SOUPS

magimix®

the possibilities are endless

JAMAICAN PUMPKIN SOUP

JAMAICAN PUMPKIN SOUP

Butternut squash makes a fine substitute for pumpkin here. Look for a yellowish plantain, if using, rather than green, as it will be sweeter and softer once roasted.

Serves 4

- 1.2kg pumpkin, peeled, deseeded and cut into 2cm cubes
- 2 tbsp light olive oil
- 1 small yellow plantain (about 150g), peeled and diced, or 150g sweet potato or pumpkin, diced
- 2 tsp fresh thyme leaves, plus a few extra to serve
- 15g butter
- 1 large red onion, thinly sliced
- 5 spring onions (white and pale green parts only), thinly sliced
- ¼–½ scotch bonnet chilli, deseeded and sliced
- 3cm piece of ginger, finely grated
- A pinch of ground allspice
- A good grating of nutmeg
- ½ tsp ground cumin
- 1.3 litres veg or chicken stock
- 1 fresh bay leaf
- Juice of 1 lime, to taste

1 Preheat the oven to 200C/gas 6. In a bowl, toss the pumpkin with half the oil and spread over a roasting tin.
2 In a separate, smaller tin, toss the plantain (or squash or pumpkin) with the remaining oil and half the thyme.
3 Season all the veg well and roast for 20-25 minutes, until everything is soft and turning golden (keep an eye on the plantain, if using, as this will be ready a few minutes before the pumpkin). Set them all aside.
4 Melt the butter in a large, heavy saucepan. Add the red onion and a pinch of salt. Partially cover with a lid and cook over a low-medium heat for 15 minutes, stirring occasionally, until the onion has softened.
5 Remove the lid and increase the heat slightly. Cook, stirring often, for 5-10 minutes, until the onion begins to turn golden. Add the spring onion, chilli, ginger, allspice, nutmeg, cumin and remaining thyme, then cook for a further 3 minutes, until fragrant.
6 Add the roasted pumpkin, veg or chicken stock and bay leaf, then bring to the boil. Cover and simmer over a low heat for 20 minutes.
7 Take off the heat, remove the bay leaf and purée the soup using a stick blender or in batches in a free-standing mixer, then return it to the saucepan. Season to taste with salt and pepper and the lime juice.
8 Warm the soup over a medium heat. Ladle into bowls and garnish with the diced plantain, sweet potato or pumpkin and the thyme.

Per serving 220 cals, 11g fat (3.4g sat fats), 4.2g protein, 28.5g carbs, 18.6g sugars

....

RED THAI SEAFOOD NOODLE SOUP

Serves 4 (DF) (GF)

- 600ml vegetable stock
- 2 lemongrass stalks, bruised
- 2-3 tsp red curry paste
- 400ml tin low-fat coconut milk
- 125g thin rice noodles
- 500g sea trout fillet, skinned and cut into chunks
- 8 large cooked peeled prawns
- Coriander sprigs, to garnish
- Lime wedges, to serve

1 Bring the stock, lemongrass, curry paste and coconut milk to the boil. Simmer for 5-6 minutes. Meanwhile, cook the noodles according to the packet instructions, then drain and keep warm. Add the trout and prawns to the soup, then simmer for 4-5 minutes, until the fish is cooked.
2 Remove the lemongrass. Divide the noodles between four bowls, ladle over the soup and garnish with the coriander and lime wedges.

Per serving 383 cals, 15g fat (6.7g sat fats), 31.2g protein, 29.3g carbs, 3g sugars

RED THAI SEAFOOD NOODLE SOUP

WATERCRESS & MINT SOUP WITH BACON SHARDS

Blanching the watercress separately may seem odd, but it preserves the flavour and colour much better. This is also delicious thinned with a little more stock and served cold on warmer days.

Serves 2

- 450g watercress, roughly chopped
- 1 large handful of mint leaves
- 20g butter
- 1 tbsp olive oil
- 2 small, sweet onions (about 280g), finely chopped
- 1 medium baking potato (about 250g), peeled and cut into very small cubes
- 650ml vegetable stock
- 4 rashers of back bacon, rind removed
- 100ml fat-free Greek yoghurt

1 Start by preparing the watercress and mint. Fill a large bowl with cold water and a handful of ice cubes, and bring a large pan of water to the boil.
2 In batches, using tongs, plunge the watercress and mint leaves, reserving a little of each to garnish, into the hot water until wilted. Transfer to the colander to drain, before immersing in the iced water to keep them nice and green. (You may need to top up the saucepan with more boiling water as you go.)
3 Heat the butter and oil in another large pan over a low-medium heat and add the onion, potato and a pinch of seasoning. Cook gently until soft but not coloured (about 10 minutes). Add the stock. Bring to just below the boil, cover and simmer for 10 minutes until tender.

4 Meanwhile, preheat the grill to medium and cook the bacon rashers for about 4 minutes, until sizzling and crisp. Set aside on kitchen paper to drain, then break it into shards.
5 Squeeze any excess water from the cooled watercress and mint, and add them to the soup. Take the pan off the heat and purée the mixture thoroughly with a hand-held stick blender - alternatively, do this in batches in a free-standing mixer, then pour it back into the pan.
6 Whisk in the yoghurt. Heat gently, stirring (don't let it boil, or it will split), and season to taste. Serve topped with the reserved watercress and mint, and the bacon shards.

Per serving 431 cals, 23.1g fat (8.4g sat fats), 22.2g protein, 36.1g carbs, 11.6g sugars

....

CHICKEN SOUP WITH SPRING VEG & PASTA

Serves 6 (DF)

(pictured p19)

- Olive oil
- 1 large onion, peeled and chopped
- 1 leek, trimmed and sliced
- 2 celery stalks, sliced
- 2 carrots, peeled and roughly chopped
- 2 courgettes, roughly chopped
- 100g orzo
- 50g frozen peas
- 200g cooked chicken, shredded
- A small bunch of fresh parsley

Chicken stock

- 1 chicken carcass and bones
- 1 large onion, peeled and quartered
- 2 carrots, scrubbed
- 2 celery stalks
- 5 black peppercorns
- A handful of parsley (optional)

1 To prepare the stock, place all of the ingredients in a large saucepan. Cover with 3 litres of cold water, then season with a little salt. Bring to the boil over a medium heat, skimming any froth off the surface with a spoon. Cover with a lid, lower the heat and simmer for 3 hours. Strain the broth through a sieve, discarding the solids, then leave it to cool.
2 To make your soup, add a splash of oil to another large saucepan and place over a medium heat. Add all the vegetables, except the peas, and sauté for 5 minutes.
3 Stir in the orzo, pour in the stock and bring to a boil. Lower the heat and simmer for 8-10 minutes, until the veg are cooked and orzo is soft, then stir in the peas and chicken until heated through. Season to taste.
4 Divide the soup between bowls, top with the herbs, and serve.

Per serving 168.3 cals, 4.3g fat (.9g sat fats), 14g protein, 19.5g carbs, 8.4g sugars

....

PEA & BASIL SOUP

(not pictured)

Serves 4 (DF) (GF) (V) (VG)

- 10 spring onions, chopped, plus extra to serve
- 750g frozen peas
- 1 litre vegetable stock
- A bunch of fresh basil, plus extra to serve

1 Heat 1 tablespoon of oil in a pan, add the spring onions and cook over a low heat for 10 minutes. Add the peas and stock; simmer for 8 minutes.
2 Add the basil then blend until smooth. Season, then serve with extra basil and spring onions.

Per serving 145 cals, 2.3g fat (0.4g sat fats), 13.2g protein, 18.6g carbs, 5.6g sugars

WATERCRESS & MINT SOUP
WITH BACON SHARDS

WINTER BEAN BROTH WITH WALNUT PESTO

a bit thick, thin it down with water. Taste and season accordingly. Stir in the pasta and simmer until the pasta is cooked, about 10-12 minutes.
3 For the pesto, heat the walnuts in the oven for 6 minutes, or until they give up some of their natural oil. Bash them in a pestle and mortar along with the garlic, basil (reserve a few pretty leaves for the garnish) and a pinch of salt. Grind into a paste and stir in enough oil to loosen.
4 Dish up the soup, adding a spoonful of pesto and a swirl of balsamic to each bowl. Scatter with the baby basil leaves and, for a bit of heat, drizzle with a little chilli sauce.

Per serving 420 cals, 21.8g fat (2.7g sat fats), 16.8g protein, 36.6g carbs, 12.4g sugars

....

CHUNKY BARLEY, LEEK & BACON SOUP
Serves 6

- 1 tbsp butter
- 1 tbsp olive oil
- 250g lean smoked bacon rashers, roughly chopped
- 4 leeks, thickly sliced
- 1 onion, peeled and thickly sliced
- 2 garlic cloves, peeled and crushed
- 200g pearl barley
- 2 large carrots, diced
- 250g butternut squash, peeled and diced
- 1 sprig of rosemary
- 1.5 litres chicken stock
- 3 tbsp finely chopped flat-leaf parsley, to serve

1 Heat the butter and olive oil in a large saucepan over a medium heat. Fry the bacon pieces for 3-4 minutes, until lightly browned, then stir in the leek, onion and garlic, and stir-fry for another 2-3 minutes.
2 Add the barley, carrot, squash, rosemary and stock. Season well and simmer gently for 45-50 minutes, or until the barley is tender. Remove the rosemary stalk, then divide the soup between wide bowls and scatter over the parsley.

Per serving 333 cals, 13.6g fat (4.8g sat fats), 16.4g protein, 38.8g carbs, 7.6g sugars

WINTER BEAN BROTH WITH WALNUT PESTO
This comforting soup is packed with veggies and creamy white beans, then finished with a chunky dollop of pesto.
Serves 4 (DF) (V) (VG)

- 400g tin cannellini beans, drained
- 1 large onion, peeled and chopped
- 2 carrots, roughly chopped
- 2 celery stalks, roughly chopped
- 2 garlic cloves, peeled and chopped
- 2 large tomatoes, roughly chopped
- 2 bay leaves
- 2 vegan stock cubes
- ½ small savoy cabbage, thinly sliced
- 2 small courgettes, thinly sliced
- A large handful of dried pasta

- Balsamic vinegar and chilli sauce (optional), to serve

Walnut pesto
- 100g walnut pieces
- 1 garlic clove, peeled
- 1 small bunch of basil, leaves picked
- Olive oil

1 Put the beans in a large pan with the onion, carrots, celery, garlic, tomatoes, bay leaves and 1.5 litres of water. Turn up the heat and simmer until the vegetables are soft and tender, about 30 minutes.
2 Preheat the oven to 170C/gas 3. Stir in the stock cubes along with the cabbage and courgettes, then simmer gently for 15 minutes. At this point, give it all a bit of a mash up to make it extra creamy and comfortingly stodgy. If it's looking

CHUNKY BARLEY, LEEK & BACON SOUP

CHICKPEA & CELERY SOUP

A rustic, Italian-style soup with a great flavour hit from the parmesan rind. When your ingredients are this simple, you want to cook them carefully, allowing the natural sweetness of the shallots and celery to shine.

Serves 2 (GF)

- 4 tbsp extra-virgin olive oil, plus extra to serve
- 4 shallots, chopped
- 2 garlic cloves, peeled and finely chopped
- 1 small head of celery (about 5 stalks), trimmed and thinly sliced (leaves reserved)
- 2 x 400g tins chickpeas, drained (or 250g dried chickpeas, soaked overnight, drained and rinsed)
- 1 fresh bay leaf
- 1 small parmesan rind (about 40g), plus grated parmesan to serve
- 1 litre veg or chicken stock

1 Gently warm the olive oil in a large saucepan, then add the shallot, garlic, celery and a pinch of salt.
2 Cook over a low heat for 15 minutes, stirring frequently, until the vegetables are soft and translucent but not coloured.
3 Increase the heat to medium, add the chickpeas, bay, parmesan rind and stock. Bring to the boil, then partially cover with a lid and simmer for 1½ hours, stirring occasionally.
4 Remove the bay and parmesan rind – they've done their job now. Spoon half the soup into a free-standing blender, blitz until smooth, then return to the pan and stir; if using a stick blender, whizz until the texture is an even mix of puréed and chunky. Season to taste.
5 Heat the soup over a medium heat, then serve with a drizzle of oil, the celery leaves and grated parmesan.
Per serving 753 cals, 39.2g fat (9g sat fats), 35g protein, 65.2g carbs, 4.2g sugars

WHOLESOME LENTIL SOUP

WHOLESOME LENTIL SOUP

Serves 4-6 (DF) (V) (VG)

- 2 onions, peeled
- 2 carrots, peeled
- 3 celery sticks
- 3 garlic cloves, peeled
- Olive oil
- A bouquet garni of thyme, bay and sage
- 225g dried green lentils
- 1 litre vegetable stock
- Crusty bread, to serve

1 Finely chop the onions, carrots, celery and garlic. Heat a drizzle of oil in a casserole pan over a medium heat, add the veg and garlic and fry for 2-3 minutes, until softened.
2 Pop in the bouquet garni, turn down the heat to low, place the lid on and let it sweat down for 10 minutes.
3 Remove the lid and pour in the lentils and stock. Simmer for 30 minutes, until the lentils are soft.
4 Remove and discard the bouquet garni, season the soup, then pour a third of it into a blender or food processor and blitz until smooth.
5 Stir the blended mixture back into the rest of the soup, loosen with a splash of water, season to taste and serve straight away with some lovely crusty bread on the side.
Per serving 241 cals, 3.3g fat (0.4g sat fats), 15.6g protein, 39.7g carbs, 9.7g sugars

PASTA

Jamie Oliver · Tefal®

MELANZANE LASAGNE

MELANZANE LASAGNE

Melanzane is the Italian word for aubergine, which forms the base of this gorgeous, creamy lasagne.

Serves 6-8 ⓥ

- 3 large aubergines, sliced into rounds
- Olive oil
- 1 tbsp oregano
- 4 garlic cloves, peeled and chopped
- ½ bunch of basil, leaves picked and stalks finely chopped
- 125ml chianti or similar Italian red wine
- 2 x 400g tins plum tomatoes
- 50g butter, plus extra for greasing
- 50g plain flour
- 800ml semi-skimmed milk
- 75g parmesan
- 300g lasagne sheets
- 125g mozzarella

1 Preheat your oven to 200C/gas 6. Place the aubergine slices in a single layer over a couple of baking trays. Drizzle with olive oil, season, and scatter over the oregano. Roast for 35-40 minutes, until the aubergine is tender and cooked through.
2 Meanwhile, make the sauce. Drizzle a glug of olive oil in a frying pan and place over a medium heat. Fry the garlic and basil stalks for 1 minute, then pour in the red wine. Bring to the boil and let it reduce down for a few minutes before adding the tinned tomatoes.
3 Bring to the boil, season well and reduce to a simmer for 10 minutes, until slightly thickened. Stir in most of the basil leaves, tearing up any larger ones, then set the rest aside. Squish the tomatoes down using the back of a spoon.
4 Melt the butter in a large non-stick pan over a medium heat. Stir in the flour and cook for a couple of minutes until you have a thick paste.
5 Gradually add the milk, whisking continuously until smooth. Cook over a low heat for about 10 minutes, stirring occasionally, until you have a thick and creamy béchamel. Finely grate in most of the parmesan,

then season. (If not using the sauce immediately, place a round piece of greaseproof paper on the surface to prevent a skin forming.)
6 Once everything is ready, grease a 25 x 25cm dish. Spoon in a third each of the roasted aubergines and tomato sauce, then cover with a layer of pasta, a third of the béchamel, then another layer of pasta. Repeat these layers twice more.
7 Once you have spread over the last layer of béchamel, grate over the rest of the parmesan and dot over the mozzarella. Scatter with the basil leaves and pop the lasagne into the oven for 40-45 minutes, until bubbling, golden and cooked through. Let it rest for 15 minutes, then serve with a salad.

Per serving 408 cals, 19.8g fat (12g sat fats), 19.6g protein, 35.8g carbs, 12.8g sugars

BLUE CHEESE & PANCETTA TAGLIATELLE

BLUE CHEESE & PANCETTA TAGLIATELLE

Serves 2

- 4 slices pancetta
- 10 spring onions, halved then sliced lengthways
- 75g blue cheese
- 200g tagliatelle

1 Bring a large pan of lightly salted water to the boil. Cook the tagliatelle as directed on the packet. Reserve a little of the cooking water.
2 Fry the pancetta until crisp. Remove from the pan and add the spring onions and fry for 2 minutes. Add the blue cheese, allow to melt, then add the tagliatelle and a splash of the cooking water. Crumble over the pancetta and serve.

Per serving 577 cals, 20.6g fat (10.9g sat fats), 24.8g protein, 78.4g carbs, 7.6g sugars

VEGGIE CARBONARA

- Olive oil
- 2 garlic cloves, peeled and finely sliced
- 1 red onion, peeled and finely chopped
- ½ celery heart, finely sliced
- 1kg mixed cherry tomatoes, halved
- 2 bay leaves
- 1 red chilli, halved lengthways
- A small bunch each of oregano, marjoram and thyme
- 1 tbsp balsamic vinegar
- 320g dried spaghetti or linguine
- 80g ricotta

1 Preheat the oven to 190C/gas 5. If you're working with larger sausages, firstly shape them into cocktail-sized ones by twisting the casing every 2-3cm and cutting to separate.
2 Set a deep, ovenproof pan or casserole over a medium heat, add a splash of olive oil and brown the sausages all over, 1-2 minutes. Then add the garlic, onion and celery, then cook slowly for about 10 minutes, or until softened.
3 Add the cherry tomatoes, bay leaves, chilli and half of each herb bunch, toss well, then pop the pan in the oven for 20 minutes.
4 Remove the pan, gently stir the mixture and tear over the remaining oregano and marjoram. Drizzle over a little olive oil and stir again.
5 Return to the oven for a further 15 minutes, until the sausages are gnarly and the tomatoes soft, then remove from the oven, gently stir in the balsamic vinegar and remove the chilli halves.
6 Meanwhile, put the pasta into a large pan of salted boiling water and cook according to the packet instructions, until it's al dente.
7 Drain the pasta, reserving some cooking water, then add to the sauce. Loosen with a little cooking water, if necessary. Serve immediately, sprinkled with small pieces of the ricotta, the remaining thyme and a drizzle of olive oil.

Per serving 778 cals, 37.5g fat (13.2g sat fats), 29.3g protein, 85.6g carbs, 17.3g sugars

VEGGIE CARBONARA
Serves 4 Ⓥ
- 400g linguine
- 4 eggs
- 2 tbsp soft ricotta cheese
- Zest of 1 lemon
- 100g fresh peas (or frozen, defrosted)
- 100g fresh baby spinach
- Green salad, to serve

1 Bring a large pan of lightly salted water to the boil. Cook the linguine according to the packet instructions.
2 Meanwhile, carefully crack the eggs into a small bowl and beat them with a fork. Season with a little black pepper, then stir in the ricotta and most of the lemon zest.
3 When the linguine has 3 minutes left, add the peas. Reserve some of the cooking water, then drain the pasta and peas and return to the pan.
4 Stir in the egg mixture and spinach with a wooden spoon – they'll cook gently in the residual heat. Add a little of the cooking water to loosen if needed.
5 Divide the carbonara between bowls and serve with a green salad.

Per serving 461 cals, 9.4g fat (2.5g sat fats), 22.2g protein, 77.5g carbs, 4.4g sugars

SLOW-COOKED TOMATO & MERGUEZ SPAGHETTI
This is a celebration of fabulously sweet tomatoes, combined here with spicy merguez sausages. Look for the best ricotta possible – we used wonderful Westcombe.
Serves 4
- 16 small merguez sausages (or 8 regular-sized ones)

SLOW-COOKED TOMATO
& MERGUEZ SPAGHETTI

SPICY SAUSAGE RAGU

PRAWN &
BROCCOLI SPAGHETTI

COURGETTE, MINT
& LEMON PENNE

SPICY SAUSAGE RAGU
Serves 4

- 2 tsp fennel seeds
- Olive oil
- 400g pork sausages, squeezed from their skins
- 1 tsp chilli flakes
- 2 x 400g tins plum tomatoes
- 1 tbsp tomato purée
- ½ bunch oregano, leaves picked
- 400g rigatoni pasta
- Parmesan, to serve

1 Using a pestle and mortar, crush the fennel seeds until fine. Place a large, wide pan over a high heat and add a drizzle of oil. Fry the sausage meat with the fennel and chilli until darkened and sticky (6–8 minutes), breaking up the meat with a spoon.
2 Stir in the tomatoes, purée and most of the oregano and simmer for 35–40 minutes, until thickened. When it's almost ready, fill a large pan with lightly salted boiling water.
3 Cook the pasta according to the packet; drain and add to the sauce, reserving a little water to loosen if needed. Serve with grated cheese and the remaining oregano on top.
Per serving 477 cals, 17.1g fat (5.3g sat fats), 19.2g protein, 66.1g carbs, 7.2g sugars.

PRAWN & BROCCOLI SPAGHETTI
Serves 4 ⓓⒻ

- 250g wholewheat spaghetti
- 300g sprouting broccoli, sliced lengthways
- 3 tbsp olive oil
- 3 garlic cloves, peeled and finely chopped
- 6 anchovy fillets in oil, chopped
- 1 tsp dried chilli flakes
- 400g raw prawns
- Grated zest and juice of 1 lemon
- 50g pine nuts, toasted
- 4 tbsp flat-leaf parsley, chopped

1 Cook the spaghetti in a large saucepan according to the packet instructions, adding the broccoli for the last 4 minutes. Drain, then return everything to the pan and set aside.
2 Heat the olive oil in a frying pan over a medium heat and fry the garlic, anchovy fillets and chilli for 1–2 minutes.
3 Stir in the prawns, lemon zest and juice, then return the pan to the heat for 3–5 minutes until the prawns are cooked through.
4 Add to the pasta and broccoli with the pine nuts and parsley. Mix well, season and serve.

Per serving 400 cals, 12.8g fat (1.9g sat fats), 30.3g protein, 43.7g carbs, 3.8g sugars

COURGETTE, MINT & LEMON PENNE
Serves 4 ⓥ

- 300g wholewheat penne
- 1 tbsp olive oil
- 3 courgettes, coarsely grated
- 2 garlic cloves, peeled and crushed
- 1–2 red chillies, deseeded and finely diced
- 200ml half-fat crème fraîche
- 4 tbsp finely chopped mint leaves
- Finely grated zest of 1 lemon
- 50g parmesan, grated

1 Cook the penne according to the packet, then drain. Heat the oil in a large pan, add the courgette, garlic and chilli. Cook over a high heat for 8 minutes, or until softened.
2 Season and stir in the crème fraîche and cook for 1 minute.
3 Remove from the heat and stir in the mint, lemon zest and parmesan. Toss the penne through the sauce with a splash of the cooking water, if needed, and serve.
Per serving 437 cals, 17g fat (8.4g sat fats), 19.1g protein, 55.5g carbs, 7.1g sugars

JAMIE'S ROTOLO
Serves 8-10 ⓥ

- 600g tipo 00 flour, plus extra for dusting
- 12 large egg yolks
- Truffle shavings (optional), to serve
- Olive oil (new season, if available), to serve

Filling
- 1 butternut squash (700g), peeled, deseeded and cut into wedges
- 100g vacuum-packed chestnuts
- 1 tsp coriander seeds
- 1 tsp fennel seeds
- 1 tsp dried red chillies
- Olive oil
- 1 leek, finely sliced
- A small handful of fresh marjoram, leaves picked (or ½ tsp dried)
- 3 garlic cloves, peeled and finely chopped
- 600g cavolo nero, stalks removed
- 2 knobs of butter
- A good grating of nutmeg
- 200g large handful of yellow girolles, cleaned
- Juice of 1 lemon
- 150g ricotta cheese, crumbled
- 55g parmesan, grated, plus extra to serve

Sage butter
- 250g butter
- 50g chestnuts, finely crumbled
- About 20 fresh sage leaves, plus extra to serve

1 Start by making your pasta dough. Place the flour in a large bowl. Make a well in the centre and tip the egg yolks into it, then beat the eggs with a fork, adding 150-200ml of cold water until smooth and not too sticky. Dust your hands with flour and knead the dough until smooth, silky and elastic, about 4 minutes. Wrap it in cling film and leave it to rest in the fridge for 30 minutes.
2 Preheat the oven to 190C/gas 5. To make the filling, place the squash wedges and chestnuts on a roasting tray. Using a pestle and mortar, bash the coriander seeds, fennel seeds and ½ teaspoon of the dried chilli along with a pinch of salt and pepper. Sprinkle this over your squash and chestnuts, drizzle over a little olive oil, then use your hands to rub it all into the vegetables.
3 Cover the tray with a damp piece of greaseproof paper and pop it in the oven for about 30 minutes. Remove the paper and let the squash roast for another 20-30 minutes, until the squash starts to caramelise. Once cool, blend until smooth in a food processor, then set aside.
4 While this is cooking, place a large pan over a medium-high heat and add 3 tablespoons of olive oil. Toss in the leek, marjoram, 2 of the garlic cloves and the remaining dried chilli. Stir and keep it moving for 20 seconds, then add the cavolo nero and a large knob of butter and cook for 15 minutes, or until softened. Grate in the nutmeg and season well, then allow to cool. Roughly chop and set aside.
5 Heat more oil in a large pan over a high heat and cook the girolles and remaining garlic for 5 minutes, until coloured, shaking the pan regularly. Add a small knob of butter and a squeeze of lemon juice, season well and set aside to cool.
6 On a clean work surface, dust both sides of your dough with flour and roll it out to the size of a tea towel (15 x 30cm), and as thin as possible, keeping it a rectangular shape and trimming as necessary. Once it's rolled out, lay your pasta sheet on a clean tea towel.
7 Spoon a line of squash along the long edge of the sheet nearest you. Sprinkle the cavolo nero mixture over the rest of the sheet, leaving the top 5cm of the pasta sheet clear. Scatter the girolles over the cavolo nero, then the ricotta and parmesan.
8 Brush the top edge of the pasta sheet with water. Working carefully, use the nearest edge of the tea towel to roll the pasta up and away from you, as tightly as possible around the squash mixture so it forms the centre. Continue to roll up the rotolo until it forms a cylinder shape. Pinch the ends flat so that the filling is not exposed.
9 Roll it tightly in the tea towel and tie it firmly at each end with kitchen string. (If you want to secure it even further tie some more round the middle.) Tie a little extra string at one end to hang out of the pan and act as a handle.
10 To cook the rotolo, fill a fish kettle or very large lidded pan with salted water and bring it to a gentle boil over a low-medium heat. Lower in the rotolo, using your fish kettle rack or place a plate on top to keep it submerged. Simmer for 25 minutes.
11 Meanwhile, make your sage butter. Fill a pan a quarter full with water and place it over a low-medium heat. Put the butter in a heatproof bowl on top of the pan and allow it to melt gently – the milky whey will sink to the bottom. Spoon out the clear golden butter and set aside. Discard the whey. (You will find that you won't need all the butter now, but it's quite hard to clarify any less than this. You can always leave the extra in the fridge to use for your roast potatoes another day.)
12 Heat 3-4 tablespoons of the clarified butter in a pan over a medium heat. Drop in a sage leaf – if it starts to sizzle around the edges, the butter is ready. Add the rest of the sage leaves and fry for 30 seconds, or until they crisp up. Take the pan off the heat, crumble in the chestnuts and toss to combine.
13 Remove the rotolo from the pan and allow it to drain on a rack for 5 minutes. Cut off the string, remove the tea towel and slice up the rotolo, then serve on a platter or individual plates. Scatter over the extra sage leaves, drizzle with the sage butter and finish with grated parmesan and shaved truffle, if you like.

Per serving 630 cals, 29.5g fat (11g sat fats), 24.1g protein, 68.9g carbs, 7.7g sugars

JAMIE'S ROTOLO

BAKED PIZZOCCHERI

This rustic pasta bake combines three cheeses with fresh greens and herbs – it's pure comfort.

Serves 6 ⓥ

- 30g butter, plus extra for greasing
- Olive oil
- 3 sprigs of sage, leaves picked
- 1 white onion, peeled and sliced
- 2 garlic cloves, peeled and finely sliced
- 200g rainbow chard, leaves stripped and finely sliced, stalks chopped separately
- 300g new potatoes, skins on, boiled and cut into 2cm chunks
- ½ radicchio, finely sliced
- 500g pizzoccheri (see note)
- 250g taleggio, chopped
- 50g parmesan, finely grated
- 100g stale breadcrumbs
- 2 sprigs of thyme, leaves picked
- 100g gorgonzola
- Mixed leaves, to serve

1 Preheat the oven to 190C/gas 5. Place a large, deep frying pan over a low heat, then add a knob of the butter, a glug of olive oil and the sage. Add the onion and garlic, then cook for 15 minutes, until soft and sticky but not coloured, adding the chard stalks for the final 5 minutes.
2 Add the potatoes, radicchio and chard leaves and cook for 2 minutes, or until the leaves have wilted.
3 Cook the pasta in a large pan of salted boiling water according to the instructions. Drain, reserving a large mug of the cooking water.
4 Stir the pizzoccheri, cooking water, taleggio and most of the parmesan into the potato mixture and stir well, so the pasta is coated in the mixture.
5 Season with a little salt and plenty of black pepper, then transfer to a buttered 30 x 20cm baking dish.
6 Blitz the breadcrumbs and thyme in a food processor, then pulse in the gorgonzola until combined. Top the pizzoccheri with the breadcrumb mixture and remaining parmesan, then bake for 25–30 minutes, until golden and crisp on the top. Serve with the mixed leaves.

SAUSAGE SPAGHETTI WITH CIME DE RAPA AFFOGATE

Note Pizzoccheri are short pieces of buckwheat tagliatelle sold in Italian delis. You can also buy online from etruscany.co.uk.
Per serving 649 cals, 24.1g fat (14.4g sat fats), 27.9g protein, 81.6g carbs, 2.6g sugars

SAUSAGE SPAGHETTI & CIME DI RAPA AFFOGATE

Affogate means 'drowned' and refers to the ingredients being immersed in the lovely pan juices. If you can't find cime di rapa, use tenderstem broccoli.

Serves 4

- 4 garlic cloves, peeled and chopped
- 1 dried red chilli, roughly chopped
- 8 tbsp olive oil
- 500g Italian-style sausages
- 500g cime di rapa, outer leaves discarded, other leaves stripped
- 400g dried spaghetti
- Grated parmesan, to finish

1 Place a large deep, lidded sauté pan over a medium heat and sweat the garlic and chilli in the oil.
2 Squeeze the sausagemeat out of its skins, break it into chunks and add to the pan. Cook until browned all over. Add the cime di rape, pour over 50ml of water, and season. Pop the lid on and cook for 15 minutes.
3 Cook the spaghetti, according to the packet instructions, in a pan of salted boiling water. Drain, reserving a splash of the cooking water, then toss the pasta and water with the sausage mixture. Serve with a drizzle of oil and grated parmesan.
Per serving 788 cals, 43.7 fat (10.9g sat fats), 34.4g protein, 67.7g carbs, 7g sugars

LEEK & CAULIFLOWER PASTA BAKE

cheese sauce and cheddar. Place the dish on a baking sheet and bake in the oven for 20–25 minutes, until golden and bubbling.

Per serving 432 cals, 21g fat (10.7g sat fats), 19.9g protein, 44.1g carbs, 14.6g sugars

SMOKY BACON, KALE & PINE-NUT PASTA

Serves 4

- 200g pack sliced curly kale
- 300g wholewheat spaghetti or linguine
- 1 tbsp olive oil
- 200g smoked-bacon lardons
- 2 garlic cloves, peeled and finely chopped
- 1 tsp dried red chilli flakes (less if you like it mild)
- 6 anchovy fillets in oil, drained and chopped
- 4 tbsp pine nuts
- 4 tbsp half-fat crème fraîche
- 1 tbsp lemon juice

1 Boil the kale in a large pan of lightly salted boiling water for 2–3 minutes or until just wilted. Drain, squeezing out any excess water with the back of a large spoon, and roughly chop.
2 Cook the linguine according to the packet instructions. Meanwhile, heat the oil in a large, non-stick frying pan over a medium-high heat and stir-fry the lardons for 4–5 minutes, until beginning to crisp. Add the garlic, chilli, anchovies and pine nuts, then stir-fry for 1–2 minutes. Throw in the kale and stir-fry for 2–3 minutes.
3 Drain the pasta, keeping some of the cooking water, then add to the pan with the crème fraîche, a splash of cooking water and the lemon juice. Toss to mix well, season with black pepper, and serve.

Per serving 464 cals, 20.5 fat (6.6g sat fats), 21.5g protein, 51.8g carbs, 4g sugars

LEEK & CAULIFLOWER PASTA BAKE

Serves 6 (v)

- 500ml tomato passata
- 1 tsp caster sugar
- ½ tsp dried red chilli flakes
- 800ml milk
- 60g plain flour
- 60g butter
- 2 tsp dijon mustard
- 100g cheddar cheese, grated
- 1 tbsp olive oil
- 3 leeks, thickly sliced
- 200g dried wholemeal penne
- 1 cauliflower, cut into florets

1 Combine the passata, sugar and chilli flakes in a medium saucepan. Season, half-cover the pan and simmer over a medium heat for 15–20 minutes, until thickened, then set aside. Meanwhile, in another saucepan, mix the milk, flour and 50g of the butter. Gently heat, whisking continuously, for 5–10 minutes until smooth, then let it bubble away for 5 minutes. Off the heat, stir in the mustard and most of the cheddar.
2 Preheat the oven to 200C/gas 6. Heat the rest of the butter with the oil in a wide frying pan and sauté the leeks over a medium heat for 6–8 minutes, until softened. Boil the pasta and cauliflower in a large pan of salted water for 10 minutes, until the pasta is al dente and the cauliflower is tender. Drain, add the leeks and toss well.
3 Pour all but 300ml of the cheese sauce into the leek mixture. Divide half of the passata in the base of an ovenproof dish and top with the leek mixture. Spoon over the remaining passata, top with the rest of the

SMOKY BACON, KALE
& PINE-NUT PASTA

WILD GARLIC GNOCCHI WITH LEMON & PECORINO
Serves 4 ⓥ

- 900g evenly sized maris piper or king edward potatoes
- 275g wild garlic
- 300g tipo 00 flour, plus extra for dusting
- 2 large egg yolks
- 75g butter
- Juice of ½ lemon
- 50g pecorino

1 Preheat your oven to 180C/gas 4. Wash the potatoes , dry well, then prick all over with a fork. Place in a roasting tray and pop in the oven for about 1 hour until cooked through.
2 Meanwhile, set a colander over a pan of boiling water, add 175g of the wild garlic and steam for 1-2 minutes. Tip into a blender and blitz into a purée. If the mixture feels too wet, spoon it into a clean tea towel and twist the edges over the sink, to remove excess moisture. Set aside.
3 As soon as the potatoes are ready, leave them to cool down just enough to handle, then carefully peel away the skins, wearing rubber gloves.
4 Push the hot potatoes through a ricer onto a clean work surface. If you don't have a ricer, use a sieve from a bit of a height and push them through with a wooden spoon.
5 Pile the flour on top of the potato, in a mound, and season generously. Make a well in the middle. Whisk the egg yolks and wild-garlic purée together, then pour it into the well.
6 Using your hands, lightly bring all the ingredients together (don't overwork the mixture or it will become tough). As soon as it comes together, clean and dry your hands and worktop for the next step.
7 Sprinkle your work surface lightly with flour, then roll out the gnocchi dough to a square, about 1cm thick. Cut into 1cm strips, then cut again to give you 2cm pieces. Shape the gnocchi by rolling them down the back of a fork to get a ridge.
8 When ready to cook your gnocchi, bring a large pan of salted water to the boil. Meanwhile, shred the remaining wild garlic leaves. Melt the butter in a large non-stick frying pan over a low heat, then add the leaves.
9 Pop the gnocchi into the boiling water for a few minutes, until they rise to the surface. Remove and add them to the pan with the wild garlic.
10 Once all the gnocchi is in the pan, stir in the lemon juice and some black pepper, grate over the pecorino, toss everything together, and serve.
Per serving 666 cals, 24.6g fat (13g sat fats), 21.6g protein, 91.2g carbs, 2.8g sugars

MUSHROOM & ARTICHOKE TAGLIATELLE

....

MUSHROOM & ARTICHOKE TAGLIATELLE
Serves 4 ⓥ

- 200g tagliatelle
- 2 tbsp olive oil
- 1 onion, peeled and finely chopped
- 3 garlic cloves, peeled and finely chopped
- 150g portobello mushrooms, finely chopped
- 50g toasted walnuts, chopped
- 150ml half-fat crème fraîche
- 100g jar artichokes, drained and chopped
- 2 tbsp chopped flat-leaf parsley
- Parmesan, grated, to serve

1 Cook the tagliatelle according to the packet. Drain, reserving some water. Heat the oil in a frying pan over a medium heat and fry the onion, garlic and mushrooms until golden. Add the walnuts, crème fraîche, artichokes and cooking water. Stir in the pasta, and top with parsley and parmesan to serve.
Per serving 430 cals, 24.8g fat (6.3g sat fats), 11.2g protein, 43.5g carbs, 6g sugars

SUMMER ORZO
SALAD WITH FETA

SUMMER ORZO SALAD WITH FETA

Serves 4 Ⓥ

- 300g orzo pasta
- Extra-virgin olive oil
- 250g cherry tomatoes on the vine
- 2 tbsp balsamic vinegar
- 350g runner beans, trimmed and sliced
- 1 small bunch of chives, finely sliced
- Juice and zest of 1 lemon
- 80g feta, crumbled
- 50g rocket

1 Preheat the oven to 180C/gas 4. Cook the orzo in a pan of boiling salted water, according to packet instructions, until al dente. Drain, then dress in a drizzle of olive oil.
2 Place the cherry tomatoes, with the vine, on a baking tray with a drizzle of olive oil, 1 tablespoon of balsamic vinegar and a pinch of salt and pepper. Roast for 15 minutes.
3 Meanwhile, cook the runner beans in a pan of boiling salted water for 2-3 minutes, until tender. Discarding the vine, mash half the tomatoes with 2 tablespoons of olive oil, the remaining tablespoon of balsamic, the chives and lemon juice to taste, season, and toss with the orzo, runner beans and lemon zest a bowl. Gently stir through the feta, remaining tomatoes and rocket to serve.

Per serving 438 cals, 15.2g fat (4.4g sat fats), 14.7g protein, 64g carbs, 10g sugars

RICOTTA RAVIOLI WITH CALABRESE RAGU

(Pictured on p29)

Use smoked ricotta here if you can find it, but any good-quality ricotta will still work wonderfully.

Serves 6

- 600g tipo 00 flour
- 6 large eggs
- Semolina flour, for dusting
- Basil leaves, to serve

Ricotta filling
- 300g ricotta (see note)
- 1 large egg
- 1 nutmeg
- 50g parmesan
- 1 lemon
- 3 sprigs of basil, leaves picked and finely chopped (optional)

Ragù
- Olive oil
- 6 Italian-style pork sausages, skins removed
- 1 white onion, peeled and finely chopped
- 1 carrot, peeled and finely chopped
- 1 celery stalk, finely chopped
- 4 garlic cloves, peeled and finely sliced
- 1 tbsp tomato purée
- 200ml dry Italian red wine
- 2 x 400g tins Italian plum tomatoes

1 Sift the flour into a very large bowl with a good pinch of fine salt. Make a well and crack the eggs into the middle. Beat them with a fork, then gradually start to mix in the flour from the sides. Once it's too hard to keep mixing with the fork, use your hands to bring it all together into a rough dough. Knead the dough for 5 minutes, or until it is smooth.
2 Roll the dough through a pasta machine until very thin, dusting with semolina as you go. Cover the dough you're not using with a damp tea towel to prevent it from drying out.
3 For the filling, place the ricotta in a large bowl and mix well until creamy. Beat the egg and add it to the ricotta, then mix again to combine. Next, grate in some nutmeg, parmesan and zest of half the lemon. Fold the chopped basil through the mixture, season to taste, then set the filling aside in the fridge until it is needed.
4 To make the ravioli, lay a sheet of pasta on a surface lightly dusted with semolina. Spoon tablespoons of the ricotta mixture onto the pasta at 10cm intervals. Dab a little cold water around the filling, then cover with another sheet of pasta.
5 Use your fingers to push out all of the air and seal the ravioli. Using a ravioli cutter or a sharp knife, slice the ravioli into 8cm squares until all of the pasta and filling is used up, transferring them to a semolina-dusted tray as you go. You should have about 24 ravioli in total.
6 To make your ragú, place a large, deep frying pan over a medium-high heat and once hot, add a good lug of olive oil. Tip in the sausage meat and cook for about 5 minutes, or until the meat is browned, breaking it up with the back of a spoon.
7 Turn the heat down to medium low and add the onion, carrot, celery and garlic, sweat for 10-15 minutes or until the veg are completely soft, then stir through the tomato purée.
8 Turn the heat up to high and pour in the wine, letting it bubble away. Add the tinned tomatoes, squashing them through your hands, along with a tin of hot water. Season well with salt and pepper, then turn the heat down and let the ragù simmer away for 1½-2 hours or until thick, reduced and delicious.
9 Boil the ravioli in a large saucepan in plenty of salted boiling water for 3 minutes, or until they float to the surface and are cooked through. Toss them in the sausage ragù, spooning more of the rich sauce over the top. Serve topped with grated parmesan and the basil leaves, if using.

Note This is best made with good-quality ricotta, such as ricotta di mucca (cow's milk ricotta), available from Italian delis or gastronomica.co.uk. If you can't get hold of the real deal, use the ricotta from the supermarket but, because it's more watery, you'll need to strain it through muslin first.

Per serving 728 cals, 25.2g fat (10.6g sat fats), 41.8g protein, 79.5g carbs, 10.5g sugars

RICE MATTERS.

DO YOUR DISH JUSTICE BY SELECTING THE NUMBER 1 PURE BASMATI*

We'd love to hear about your favourite recipe:
🐦 @TildaBasmati   f TildaRice   #RiceMatters

*IRI, Total UK, 52 w/e 12 Sept, 2015

RICE & GRAINS

Tilda®
Legendary Rice

**SWEET POTATO &
WHITE BEAN CHILLI**

Basmati rice's gentle fragrance and long, slender grains means it is sometimes referred to as the 'prince of rice'. Tilda Pure Basmati grains consistently cook up light and fluffy and bring a distinctive, slightly 'nutty' taste to any meal. Rinse your rice before cooking – this removes excess starch and brings out maximum flavour. Whether you're pairing it with fragrant spices or creamy sauces, Tilda Pure Basmati works in harmony with your recipes

SWEET POTATO & WHITE BEAN CHILLI

Serves 4-6 ⒟Ⓕ ⒼⒻ Ⓥ ⓋⒼ

- 2 medium sweet potatoes, peeled and chopped
- 2 tbsp olive oil
- 2 tsp ground cinnamon
- 1 tbsp ground cumin
- 1 tsp smoked paprika
- 1 onion, peeled and chopped
- 1 bunch of coriander, leaves picked and stalks chopped
- 1 red chilli, chopped
- 2 red peppers and 1 yellow pepper, chopped
- 400g tin cannellini beans
- 400g tin tomatoes
- Cooked basmati rice, to serve
- Guacamole, to serve (optional)

1 Preheat the oven to 180C/gas 4. Toss the sweet potato with 1 tablespoon of olive oil and a pinch each of the cinnamon, cumin and paprika. Roast in the oven for 35–40 minutes, then set aside.
2 Heat 1 tablespoon of oil in a large pan and add the onion, coriander stalks, chilli and peppers along with the remaining spices. Cook, stirring, over a low heat, for 15 minutes.
3 Add the cannellini beans with their liquid, and the tinned tomatoes. Stir, adding a splash of water to loosen, if needed. Simmer for 30 minutes, then stir in the sweet potatoes along with most of the coriander leaves.
4 Season to taste, top with the rest of the coriander leaves. Serve over rice with the guacamole on the side.
Per serving 358 cals, 8.6g fat (1.6g sat fats), 12.4g protein, 56.9g carbs, 20.5g sugars

....

KYLIE KWONG'S AMAZING FRIED EGGS WITH RICE

This is a great dish from renowned Sydney chef Kylie - fried eggs go so brilliantly with the black rice.
Serves 4 ⒟Ⓕ ⒼⒻ

- 300g black rice
- 200g mixed chard, leaves picked, stalks finely sliced
- A drizzle of sesame oil
- A thumb-sized piece of ginger, peeled and grated

KYLIE KWONG'S AMAZING FRIED EGGS WITH RICE

- 6 spring onions
- A squeeze of lemon juice
- Sunflower oil, for deep-frying
- 8 large eggs
- 2 garlic cloves, peeled and finely sliced
- Oyster sauce
- Ground white pepper
- 2 tbsp sesame seeds, toasted
- ½ small bunch of coriander, leaves picked
- 2 bird's-eye chillies, finely sliced

1 Cook the black rice according to the packet. Add the chard stalks 5 minutes towards the end, and the leaves for the last 30 seconds.
2 Drain, then stir in the sesame oil, ginger, two of the spring onions, finely sliced, and the lemon juice.
3 Place a non-stick wok over a high heat and pour in 2cm of sunflower oil. Once the oil is really hot, crack in the eggs, four at a time, and deep-fry until the whites are crispy around the edges but the yolks are runny. Add the sliced garlic to the wok halfway through and cook until crispy.
4 Using the back of a spoon, smear some oyster sauce over half of each plate, then spoon a mound of the rice and chard mixture on the other side. Mould it with a teacup if you fancy.
5 With a fish slice or slotted spoon, remove the eggs, draining off any excess oil, then place two on each plate, on the sauce. Sprinkle with a little white pepper.
6 Finely slice the remaining spring onions and scatter over the dish with the sesame seeds, coriander leaves and chillies. Serve immediately.
Per serving 591 cals, 30.3g fat (5.9g sat fats), 23.1g protein, 56.1g carbs, 2g sugars

**GIANT COUSCOUS WITH
HALLOUMI & BEETROOT**

- 50g almonds, skinned or unskinned
- A generous pinch of saffron threads
- 5 sprigs of thyme, leaves picked
- 2 tomatoes, chopped
- 4 large skinless chicken thighs, boned and cut into pieces
- 300g cooking chorizo, chopped
- 1 onion, peeled and finely chopped
- 200g wild mushrooms, such as oyster or chanterelle, any larger ones cut into pieces
- 500g spanish paella rice, such as calasparra or bomba (see note)

1 Heat the olive oil in a large ovenproof casserole dish or pan (ideally a terracotta dish). Add the garlic and almonds and fry for 3-5 minutes, until golden.
2 Remove from the pan and mix in the saffron, thyme and tomato. Tip all of the mixture into a food processor and blitz into a smooth paste. Set aside until needed.
3 Season the chicken with a little salt and add to the pan with the chorizo. Fry over a high heat until dark golden, 3-5 minutes, then add the onion and cook, stirring, for 5 minutes. Add the mushrooms and sauté for a further 5 minutes.
4 By now, the meat and onions should be fairly brown. Add the saffron paste and cook, stirring, for 3-4 minutes, then pour in 1.5 litres of boiling water. Bring back to the boil and simmer for 20 minutes, until you have a rich stock. In the meantime, preheat the oven to 220C/gas 7.
5 Add the rice to the pan and cook, stirring occasionally, for about 10 minutes, then put the whole pan in the oven for a further 8-10 minutes. Turn the oven off, open the door and leave the pan in the oven to rest for 5 minutes. Transfer to a serving dish and serve straight away.
Note You can buy bomba rice at most supermarkets and calasparra rice is available at brindisa.com.
Per serving 521 cals, 25g fat (6g sat fats), 21g protein, 53g carbs, 3g sugars

GIANT COUSCOUS WITH HALLOUMI & BEETROOT
Serves 4 ⓥ
- 250g wholewheat giant couscous
- Olive oil
- Juice of 1½ oranges
- 2 garlic cloves, peeled and crushed
- 1-2 tsp runny honey
- Juice of 2 limes
- 200g halloumi, cut into slices
- 2 large handfuls each of chopped coriander and mint leaves
- 300g cooked baby beetroot, quartered

1 Bring a pan of lightly salted water to the boil, add the couscous and simmer for 6-8 minutes, or until tender. Drain and transfer to a bowl with 2 tablespoons of olive oil and the orange juice.

2 In a separate bowl, combine 4 tablespoons of olive oil with the garlic, honey, and lime juice. Whisk to combine, then set aside. Brush the halloumi with oil then place on a hot, non-stick griddle, in batches, for 2-3 minutes, until golden, turning once.
3 Fluff up the couscous with a fork, add the garlic honey mixture and toss to combine. Transfer to a serving dish and stir in the herbs and beetroot. Top with the halloumi and serve.
Per serving 545 cals, 27.7g fat (11.3g sat fats), 21.4g protein, 55.7g carbs, 11.2g sugars

....

ARROZ A LA AMPURDANESA
(Catalonian-style rice)
Serves 8 ⓓⒻ
- 70ml olive oil
- 5 garlic cloves, peeled

SPICED BURGER WITH
HOUMOUS & ONION RELISH

quinoa with the dates, mustard, jam, 2 tablespoons of olive oil and a pinch of pepper. Blitz the mixture in a food processor until combined, then stir in the reserved beans and quinoa. Shape the mixture into six patties.
4 Preheat the oven to 200C/gas 6. For the houmous, mix all the spices along with 3 tablespoons of the oil. Toss the cauliflower in a roasting tray with the spice mix and roast for 30 minutes, or until golden.
5 In a food processor, blend the roasted cauliflower with the chickpeas, tahini, garlic and the remaining 3 tablespoons of olive oil, until smooth (add a splash of water if needed). Season to taste.
6 For the relish, heat the oil in a frying pan and cook the onion until soft and sticky, about 20 minutes. If it dries out, add a splash of water. Spoon into a bowl and drizzle with pomegranate molasses.
7 To cook the burgers, add olive oil to your onion pan and fry on each side for about 6 minutes, until crispy on the outside and hot in the middle.
8 To serve, layer everything up in the buns with the tomato, tomato relish and your favourite salad leaves.
Per serving 522 cals, 27g fat (3.8g sat fats), 18.1g protein, 55.2g carbs, 21g sugars

SPICED BURGER WITH HOUMOUS & ONION RELISH
Serves 6 (DF) (V) (VG)
- 100g uncooked quinoa (200g cooked weight)
- 400g tin of black beans, drained
- 1 tsp ground cumin
- 1 tbsp sweet smoked paprika
- 1 tbsp ground coriander
- 4 large, juicy dates
- 2 tbsp French's yellow mustard
- 2 tbsp apricot jam
- Olive oil
- Wholemeal buns, sliced tomato, tomato relish and salad leaves, to serve

Houmous
- 1 tbsp ground cumin
- 1 tbsp ground coriander
- 1 tbsp sweet smoked paprika
- 1 tsp chilli powder
- 6 tbsp olive oil
- 1 small cauliflower, broken into florets
- 400g jar of chickpeas, drained
- 3 tbsp tahini
- ½ garlic clove

Onion relish
- A splash of olive oil
- 1 large onion, peeled and chopped
- Drizzle of pomegranate molasses

1 Toast the uncooked quinoa in a pan over a low–medium heat, until you hear it start to crackle and pop. Then cook the quinoa according to the packet. When all the water is absorbed, keep it in the pan with the heat on until you can hear it crackle again. This will give you a firm patty.
2 Tip the black beans into a frying pan with the spices and dry-toast for 2 minutes, until they pop.
3 Mix half the beans and half the

KALE, POMEGRANATE & FARRO SALAD
Serves 4 as a side (V)
- 150g kale, stalks removed
- 1 lemon, halved
- 125g farro
- 1 pomegranate, seeds only
- 75g feta
- Extra-virgin olive oil

1 Place the kale in a bowl with a pinch of salt and the juice of a lemon half, scrunch it together and set aside.
2 In a medium saucepan, cook the farro according to the packet. Add to the kale along with the pomegranate seeds. Crumble in the feta, drizzle with oil and the remaining lemon juice, season and serve.
Per serving 191 cals, 6.6g fat (3g sat fats), 8.1g protein, 24.1g carbs, 2.2g sugars

KALE, POMEGRANATE
& FARRO SALAD

#1 RICE FOR ALL OCCASIONS

Tilda rice is the ultimate store cupboard essential. Their naturally gluten-free, versatile Pure Basmati rice is perfect for all occasions: whether you're looking to create a show-stopping dinner party dish; choose a healthy wholegrain alternative to keep you feeling full for longer; make a nutritious meal for little ones; or prepare a quick and tasty side dish.

Savoury or sweet, hot or cold, Tilda Basmati rice is delicious, nutritious, gorgeously aromatic and elevates almost any dish. Each of Tilda's varieties offer a distinctive flavour and texture that can be matched perfectly with recipes and ingredients from around the world.

To ensure your Basmati rice is always light and fluffy, Tilda removes any broken and discoloured grains to ensure that only the purest Basmati makes its way on to your plate.

For more delicious recipe ideas visit tilda.com, or try our pilau, far right

QUINOA & ROAST VEG

QUINOA & ROAST VEG
Serves 4-6 (GF) (V)
- 2 yellow peppers, deseeded and diced
- 6 baby courgettes, halved
- 2 red onions, peeled and diced
- 200g cherry tomatoes
- 4 tbsp olive oil
- 200g quinoa
- 3 tbsp basil pesto
- 400g tin chickpeas, drained and rinsed
- 15 black olives, destoned
- 100g goat's cheese, crumbled
- A handful of flat-leaf parsley, chopped

1 Preheat the oven to 200C/gas 6, then place the peppers, courgettes, red onions and tomatoes in a roasting dish. Season, drizzle with 2 tablespoons of the olive oil, then roast in the oven for 20-25 minutes.
2 Meanwhile, cook the quinoa according to the packet instructions and keep warm. Remove the veg from the oven and transfer to a serving plate. Tip all the tray juices into a bowl with the pesto and remaining oil, then mix well.
3 Toss the quinoa with the roasted veg, chickpeas and olives. Pour over the pesto mixture, season and toss to mix. Scatter with the cheese and parsley to serve.
Per serving 630 cals, 36.7g fat (8.8g sat fats), 23g protein, 54.2g carbs, 12.7g sugars

FENNEL RISOTTO
(pictured p47)
Serves 4-6 (GF)
- 1.4 litres chicken stock
- 2 fennel bulbs, with fronds

Tilda ®
Legendary Rice

- 2 knobs of butter
- Olive oil
- 1 tsp dried chilli flakes
- 1 large onion, peeled and finely chopped
- 4 stalks of celery, finely chopped
- 2 garlic cloves, peeled and finely chopped
- 450g arborio risotto rice
- 90ml vodka
- 50g parmesan, grated
- Finely grated zest and juice of 1 lemon
- Extra-virgin olive oil
- 30g pine nuts, toasted and crushed
- A pinch of fennel seeds

1 Pour your stock into a pan over a low heat and leave on a low simmer. Cut each fennel bulb into eight wedges, reserving the fronds and keeping them in cold water for later.
2 Preheat a medium-sized non-stick pan and add 1 knob of butter, a splash of olive oil, the chilli flakes, fennel and 120ml of the hot stock. Place a damp piece of greaseproof paper snugly on top, followed by the lid, and cook for 40 minutes, or until the fennel is soft, sweet and slightly caramelised.
3 Meanwhile, put the onion, celery and garlic in a high-sided pan over a low-medium heat, along with 1 tablespoon of oil. Cook, stirring occasionally, for 15 minutes, or until softened but not coloured.
4 Add the rice and stir for a couple of minutes, then turn the heat up to medium–high. Pour in the vodka and let it cook away completely. Stir in the remaining stock, a ladleful at a time, allowing each to be almost absorbed before adding the next.
5 Cook, stirring regularly, for 15 minutes or until the rice is done but still holds its shape. Add a final splash of stock to loosen, then stir in the caramelised fennel mixture.
6 Remove from the heat and beat in the second knob of butter. Stir in the parmesan, lemon zest and juice,

then season. Cover and leave to sit for 2 minutes, then stir well.
7 Finish with a drizzle of extra-virgin olive oil and serve straight away, scattering over the pine nuts, fennel seeds and fennel fronds.

Per serving 746 cals, 22.8g fat (8.4g sat fats), 25.8g protein, 96g carbs, 6.3g sugars

SPICED BEEF & RICE HOTPOT
(not pictured)
Serves 4

- 3 tbsp oil
- 400g stewing beef, cut into small cubes
- 4 garlic cloves, peeled and chopped
- 4cm piece of ginger, peeled and finely chopped
- 2 tbsp curry paste of your choice
- 250g long-grain rice, rinsed until the water runs clear
- 375ml stock
- 2 large onions, sliced
- 2 carrots, cut into matchsticks
- 12 curry leaves
- Plain yoghurt and chilli, to serve (optional)

1 Heat 1 tablespoon oil in a large pan and brown the beef. Stir in the garlic, ginger and curry paste to coat the meat, and cook for 1–2 minutes. Add 200ml water, cover and very gently cook for 45–50 minutes or until the liquid has reduced. Add the rice, then the stock. Cover and cook on the lowest heat for 30 minutes or until all of the liquid has been absorbed
2 Off the heat, allow it to sit for 20 minutes, tightly covered. Heat the remaining oil and slowly sweat the onions for about 10 minutes
3 Add the carrots and curry leaves and cook for 10 minutes, until golden. Fluff up the rice with a fork and stir through the veg. Serve with a dollop of yoghurt and some chopped chilli on top.

Per serving 501 cals, 14.9g fat (2.7g sat fats), 29.7g protein, 61.9g carbs, 8.2g sugars

BAKED CHICKEN & CHORIZO PILAU
Serves 4

- 4 tbsp light olive oil
- 6 boneless chicken thighs, halved
- 200g chorizo, cut into 4cm cubes
- 1 red onion finely sliced
- 2 garlic cloves, finely chopped
- 200g cherry tomatoes
- 300g Tilda Wholegrain Basmati
- 7-8 strands of saffron
- 1.4 litres chicken stock
- 4 tbsp finely chopped parsley

1 Preheat the oven to 200C/gas 6. Add the olive oil to a lidded hob-proof oven dish. Sauté the chorizo and chicken until golden, then remove and set aside.
2 Add the onions, garlic and tomatoes to the oils left in the dish, stir to coat, then pop in the oven for 15 minutes.
3 Reduce the oevn to 180C/gas 4. Rinse and drain the rice then add to the pan with the chicken, chorizo, saffron and stock. Cover and bake for 30 more minutes.
4 If very dry after 20 minutes, add 100ml water, cover and return to the oven. When ready, scatter over the parsley, season and serve.

BRILLIANT BRASSICAS

with love your greens

TASTY

HEALTHY

SUPER-COOL CAULIFLOWER

SMASHING SWEDE

CRACKING CABBAGE

SUPER SPROUTS

TERRIFIC TURNIP

UN-BEATABLE BROCCOLI

WWW.LOVEYOURGREENS.CO.UK

GREAT RECIPES

FREE RESOURCES

FUN FACTS

Campaign financed with aid from the European Union and the
Brassica Growers Association/Horticultural Development Company

SALAD & VEG

love your
greens

GADO-GADO

GADO-GADO
Serves 4 (DF)

- 400g red potatoes
- 230g purple sprouting broccoli, tough stalks trimmed
- 1 tbsp sesame oil
- 200g brussels sprouts, thickly sliced
- 200g silken tofu, thickly sliced
- 8 quail eggs
- ¼ red cabbage, finely sliced
- 12 radishes, halved, tops reserved
- A bunch of coriander, picked
- 100g bean sprouts, to serve
- Prawn crackers, to serve (optional)

Sauce

- 120g crunchy peanut butter
- 50g palm sugar, grated
- 1 tbsp low-salt soy sauce
- 1 tbsp tamarind paste
- 2 tsp fish sauce
- 1-2 red chillies
- 1 garlic clove
- Zest and juice of 2 limes

1 To make the sauce, put all of the ingredients in a blender and blitz until smooth, adding a splash of water to loosen if needed. Pour it into a large pan, stir in 150-200ml of water and set aside.
2 Bring a pan of water to the boil over a medium heat and cook the potatoes for 15 minutes, until just cooked, adding the broccoli for the last 5 minutes. Drain, allow to cool, then slice the potatoes 1cm thick.
3 Add a splash of the sesame oil to a large frying pan and stir-fry the brussels sprouts over a medium-high heat for 6-8 minutes, until golden. Remove from the pan and set aside.
4 Heat the remaining sesame oil in the same pan over a medium heat. Fry the tofu for 4-6 minutes, until golden brown, flipping it halfway.
5 Boil the eggs in a pan of salted water over a medium heat for 1½ minutes. Leave to cool in a bowl of iced water.

RAINBOW SLAW WITH TAHINI DRESSING & SESAME SEEDS

6 Toss all the veg and tofu in the sauce. Peel and slice the eggs and arrange on top. Mix everything together with the bean sprouts, scatter on the coriander and serve with the prawn crackers, if using.
Per serving 483 cals, 24.3g fat (4.8g sat fats), 25.6g protein, 42.1g carbs, 20.6g sugars

RAINBOW SLAW WITH TAHINI DRESSING & SESAME SEEDS
Serves 4 (DF) (V) (VG)

- ¼ savoy cabbage (200g)
- 200g runner beans, peeled into ribbons
- 2 courgettes, green or yellow, peeled into ribbons
- 1 carrot, peeled into ribbons
- 1 red chilli, finely sliced
- 1 tbsp sesame seeds, toasted
- A few sprigs of coriander, leaves picked

Dressing

- 2 tbsp extra-virgin olive oil
- Juice of 1 lime, plus wedges to serve
- 2 tsp tahini
- 2 tsp light soy sauce

1 Start by finely slicing the cabbage (using a mandoline - with the guard - if you have one). Put it into a large bowl with the runner beans, courgette, carrot and chilli.
2 Mix together the dressing ingredients and season. Pour over the salad and massage in. Leave to marinate for 5 minutes, before topping with the sesame seeds and coriander. Serve with lime wedges.
Per serving 127 cals, 8.9g fat (1.4g sat fats), 4.8g protein, 7.4g carbs, 6.6g sugars

AVOCADO, GRAPEFRUIT
& ROCKET SALAD

- A thumb-sized piece of ginger, roughly chopped
- 3 garlic cloves, peeled and chopped
- 4 tbsp smooth peanut butter
- 2 tsp tamarind paste
- 1 red onion, peeled and chopped
- 1 red chilli, sliced

Temper
- A glug of groundnut oil
- 2 banana shallots, peeled and very thinly sliced
- 2 garlic cloves, peeled and very thinly sliced
- 1 long red chilli, very thinly sliced
- 1 tsp yellow mustard seeds
- A small bunch of dried curry leaves
- A handful of peanuts, crushed

1 Preheat the oven to 190C/gas 5. To make the paste, gently and briefly heat the spices in a dry frying pan, until fragrant. With a blender, spice grinder or pestle and mortar, blend them with the other paste ingredients until combined.
2 Rub half of the paste on the aubergines, getting it into all the cracks. Put in a roasting tray, cover in foil and roast, skin-side down, for 20 minutes, then remove the foil and cook for 20–30 minutes, until the aubergines are a little charred on the edges and juicy in the middle.
3 Meanwhile, heat a little oil in a medium-sized pan, then slowly fry the onion until very soft and sticky. Add the remaining paste and the coconut milk, then gently heat through, slowly stirring until you have a delicious sauce. Pour into a serving bowl and set aside.
4 For the temper, pour the oil in a frying pan and slowly fry the shallots, garlic and chilli until they start to get crispy, about 6 minutes. Add the mustard seeds, curry leaves and peanuts. Fry until everything's sizzling and crispy, about 2 minutes.
5 Scatter the temper over the aubergines and serve with the sauce, brown rice, pickles, poppodoms, salad and lime wedges.

Per serving 274 cals, 19.5g fat (7.4g sat fats), 8.1g protein, 18.2g carbs, 5.3g sugars

AVOCADO, GRAPEFRUIT & ROCKET SALAD

Serves 4 DF GF V
- 2 pink grapefruit, cut into segments
- 2 avocados, peeled, stoned and sliced
- 100g wild rocket
- 6 tbsp olive oil
- 2 tbsp sherry vinegar
- 1 tbsp honey

1 Place the grapefruit segments in a large salad bowl along with the avocado and rocket.
2 Make a dressing by shaking up the remaining ingredients in a jam jar until combined. Season to taste, then pour over the salad and serve.

Per serving 333 cals, 29.5g fat (4.9g sat fats), 2.7g protein, 14.2g carbs, 13g sugars

ROASTED AUBERGINE & PEANUT CURRY

A gorgeous veggie curry packed with flavour and warming spices. Serve everything in the middle of the table and let everyone tuck in!

Serves 6 DF GF V VG
- 4 large aubergines, halved lengthways, flesh scored in a criss-cross pattern
- Groundnut oil
- 1 large brown onion, peeled and thinly sliced
- 400ml tin low-fat coconut milk
- Brown rice, pickle, poppadoms, salad and lime wedges, to serve

Spice paste
- 1 tsp turmeric
- 1 tsp ground cumin
- 1 tsp ground coriander
- 1 tsp chilli powder

ROASTED AUBERGINE &
PEANUT CURRY

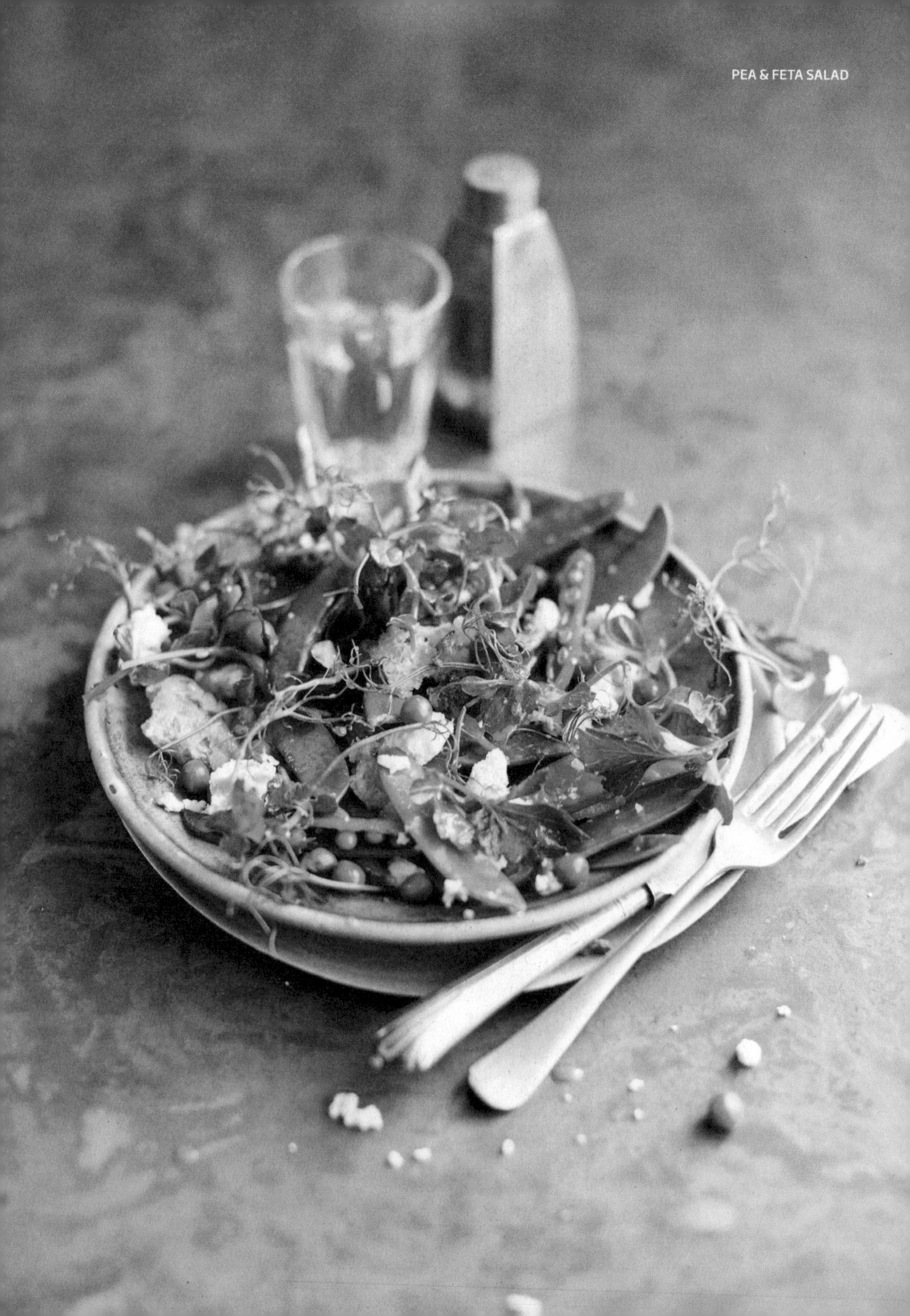

PEA & FETA SALAD
Serves 4 as a side ⓥ
- 1 garlic clove, peeled
- Extra-virgin olive oil
- 75g ciabatta, torn or sliced into small pieces
- 150g fresh peas (or frozen peas, defrosted)
- 100g mangetout
- 100g sugar snap peas
- A small bunch of parsley, leaves picked
- 75g pea shoots
- 130g feta, crumbled

Dressing
- 3 tbsp extra-virgin olive oil
- 1 tbsp red wine vinegar
- 1 tsp dijon mustard
- ¼ tsp sugar

1 Preheat the oven to 190C/ gas 5. Crush the garlic in a pestle and mortar with a good glug of oil. Toss and scrunch the bread in the garlicky oil on a baking tray. Season with salt.
2 Bake for 20 minutes, tossing halfway, until golden and crisp. Remove and leave to cool slightly.
3 Blanch the peas (not if using frozen), mangetout and sugar snaps in boiling salted water for 2–3 minutes, then drain and plunge into ice-cold water.
4 In a lidded jar, shake up the dressing ingredients with a pinch each of salt and pepper. Arrange the salad on a platter (if using frozen peas, add them here), crumble over the feta last, and gently toss together with the dressing.
Per serving 266 cals, 17.3g fat (5.3g sat fats), 11.1g protein, 17.4g carbs, 4.1g sugars

....

STUFFED ARTICHOKES
Serves 4
- 6 medium artichokes (about 1kg)
- 1 slice of lemon, plus a grating of lemon zest
- Olive oil
- 100g formaggio di fossa (see note)
- 4 slices parma ham
- 2 garlic cloves, peeled and sliced
- 3 sprigs of thyme, leaves picked

STUFFED ARTICHOKES

- 250g stale ciabatta, blitzed into breadcrumbs
- 80g parmesan, finely grated, plus extra for serving

1 Peel the tough outer leaves from the artichokes, remove the choke and stalk then trim the tops. Cook in a large pan of salted boiling water, along with the lemon slice, for 15–20 minutes or until al dente (you don't want them too soft yet). Drain, then place in a snug baking dish, about 30 x 20cm, and drizzle with oil.
2 Preheat the oven to 200C/gas 6. Cut the formaggio di fossa into 2cm slices and tuck evenly between the leaves of the artichokes. Set aside.
3 Place the parma ham on a baking tray and pop in the oven for about 5 minutes, or until crisp. Remove and turn the oven down to 180C/gas 4.
4 Place a large frying pan over a medium heat. Add a splash of oil, the garlic and thyme leaves, then fry for 1–2 minutes, until golden.
5 Add the breadcrumbs and cook for 3 minutes, until golden. Tip into a food processor, along with the parma ham, parmesan and lemon zest, then blitz until fine. Season to taste, if needed.
6 Stuff the artichokes with the breadcrumb mix. Drizzle with a little more oil and bake in the oven for 20–30 minutes, until the artichokes are tender and the topping is golden and crisp. Grate over a little extra parmesan, then serve.
Note Formaggio di fossa is a strong sheep's milk cheese. Find it in Italian delis or at finefoodspecialist.co.uk
Per serving 432 cals, 20g fat (9.8g sat fats), 28.6g protein, 40.4g carbs, 5.7g sugars

STEAMED VEG SALAD WITH MUSTARD VINAIGRETTE

bowl, gently toss in the dressing and transfer to a platter, or serve the dressing on the side for dipping.
5 Top with the goat's cheese and the borage (if using), then serve the veg warm with slices of brown bread.
Note Borage flowers are in season from May to September. Buy flowers from finefoodspecialist.co.uk or plants from victoriananursery.co.uk.
Per serving 131 cals, 10.1g fat (2.9g sat fats), 5g protein, 5.4g carbs, 4g sugars

....

COURGETTE TRIFOLIATE
Serves 8-10 as antipasti ⓥ

* Olive oil
* 4 garlic cloves, peeled and sliced
* A few sprigs of basil, leaves picked, stalks finely chopped
* 500g small courgettes, halved lengthways and sliced into 1cm half moons
* 150g cherry tomatoes
* A pinch of dried chilli flakes
* Juice of ½ lemon
* 1 ciabatta loaf, cut into 2cm slices
* 100g salted ricotta (optional)

1 Place a large non-stick pan on a medium heat and pour in a glug of olive oil. Add the garlic and basil stalks, then, after 1 minute, add the courgette slices. Stir everything together and fry for a few minutes before reducing the heat to low.
2 Season well, add the tomatoes and chilli flakes, then sauté the veg for about 1 hour, stirring often, until the courgettes are soft and the mixture has thickened.
3 Add the lemon juice along with most of the basil leaves, then check the seasoning.
4 Place a griddle pan over a high heat or preheat the grill to high. Griddle each side of the ciabatta until nicely toasted, then arrange on a board.
5 Drizzle with olive oil, spread on the sautéed courgettes and serve straight away, sprinkled with the remaining basil and shavings of salted ricotta, if you like.
Per serving 138 cals, 4.2g fat (1.3g sat fats), 62g protein, 20.1g carbs, 3g sugars

STEAMED VEG SALAD WITH MUSTARD VINAIGRETTE
Serves 4 ⓥ

* 3 shallots, peeled and thinly sliced
* ½ small bunch each of chervil and tarragon, leaves picked
* 1 tbsp white wine vinegar
* 2 tsp dijon mustard
* 1 tbsp walnut oil
* 1 tbsp extra-virgin olive oil
* 2 bunches of fine asparagus (about 20 spears), trimmed
* 1 small bunch of baby carrots (about 8), trimmed
* 1 bunch of leafy radishes (about 8), leaves intact
* 1 bunch of beetroot leaves (optional)
* 1 bunch of rainbow chard
* 50g crumbly goat's cheese

* A handful of borage flowers (optional, see note)
* Brown bread, to serve

1 To make the vinaigrette, place the shallots in a small bowl. Finely chop half the chervil and tarragon leaves, then add to the bowl. Put the remaining leaves to one side.
2 Add the vinegar, dijon mustard and oils to the bowl and season. Mix well, taste and adjust if needed. Set aside.
3 Set a three-tiered bamboo steamer over a large pan of simmering water. Put the asparagus and carrots in the bottom tier, add the radishes to the second tier then place the beetroot leaves and chard in the top one. Pop the lid on and steam for 10-15 minutes, until the leaves and vegetables are tender.
4 Tip the veg into a large shallow

SUPER SPROUT FRITTERS

BRAISED RUNNER BEAN
& TOMATO STEW

SUPER SPROUT FRITTERS
Brussels sprouts are not just for Christmas! That said, this is ideal for using up leftovers on Boxing Day. This recipe works with all sorts of veggies.
Makes 12 fritters (GF) (V)

- 250g cooked brussels sprouts, shredded
- 2 handfuls (about 100g) of cooked green veg, shredded
- 50g soft cheese, such as brie
- ½ garlic clove, peeled and finely chopped
- 1 tbsp chopped dill
- Finely grated zest of 1 lemon
- 3 large eggs

1 Put the shredded sprouts and greens into a bowl. Crumble in the cheese, add the garlic, dill and lemon zest and a good pinch of salt and pepper, and mix well. Crack in the eggs and mix to combine.
2 Place a large frying pan over a medium heat and add a generous glug of olive oil. Once the oil is hot, carefully lower in heaped tablespoons of the mixture and flatten them out into little patties.
3 Fry for 2–3 minutes, until the egg is beginning to set, then carefully flip and fry on the other side for 2 more minutes, until the egg is completely cooked.
4 Serve the fritters straight away, with a green salad, if you like.
Per serving 62 cals, 5g fat (1.7g sat fats), 3.9g protein, 0.7g carbs, 0.6g sugars

BRAISED RUNNER BEAN & TOMATO STEW
This works brilliantly as a side dish to grilled chicken or fish, although we love it on its own with some crusty bread on the side to mop up the delicious sauce.
Serves 4 (DF) (GF) (V) (VG)

- 2 tbsp olive oil
- 1 large white onion, peeled and finely sliced
- 2 garlic cloves, peeled and finely chopped
- 400g runner beans, sliced
- 2 x 400g tins plum tomatoes
- A pinch of dried oregano
- A few sprigs of chervil
- Extra-virgin olive oil
- Balsamic vinegar, to taste

1 Heat the oil in a large, deep-sided pan over a medium heat and cook the onion for 10 minutes to soften. Add the garlic for 2 minutes, then the beans. Stir in the plum tomatoes, plus half a tin of water, breaking them up with the back of your spoon. Add the oregano and season.
2 Bring to a simmer and turn the heat down to low. Place a lid on and leave for 35–40 minutes. Cook until the beans are tender and cooked through, and the sauce is thick and rich. Divide between four plates, then top with small sprigs of chervil and a drizzle each of olive oil and balsamic vinegar.
Per serving 152 cals, 9g fat (1.3g sat fats), 4.8g protein, 14g carbs, 10.8g sugars

CHILLI RUNNER BEANS
WITH ALMOND DUKKAH

CATALONIAN AUBERGINE
& WALNUTS

CHILLI RUNNER BEANS WITH ALMOND DUKKAH

Dukkah is a blend of nuts, seeds, herbs and spices

Serves 4 (DF) (GF) (V) (VG)

- 2 tbsp olive oil
- 1 garlic clove, peeled and thinly sliced
- 1 red chilli, thinly sliced
- 500g runner beans

Dukkah

- 20g sesame seeds
- 20g almonds, skin on
- 1 tsp cumin seeds
- 1 tsp coriander seeds
- ½ tsp fennel seeds

1 To make the dukkah, toast all the ingredients in a small frying pan over a medium heat for 2-3 minutes, until lovely and fragrant.
2 Tip into a mortar along with a pinch of sea salt and coarsely grind with the pestle.
3 In a small frying pan, heat the oil, fry the garlic and chilli in it until golden, then remove the pan from the heat. Blanch the beans in a pan of boiling salted water for 2-3 minutes, then drain and pat dry.
4 Place a griddle pan over a high heat, and griddle the beans for 4-5 minutes until charred and tender, turning halfway through. Remove and toss in the chilli and garlic oil. Scatter over the dukkah.
Per serving 144 cals, 12.6g fat (1.8g sat fats), 4.5g protein, 4.7g carbs, 3.9g sugars

CATALONIAN AUBERGINE & WALNUTS

Serves 6 (DF) (GF) (V) (VG)

- 6 tbsp olive oil
- 1kg aubergines, chopped
- 1 red onion, peeled and sliced
- 3 garlic cloves, peeled and finely chopped
- 3 tbsp chopped flat-leaf parsley
- 1 tsp sweet smoked paprika
- 600g tomatoes, peeled, deseeded and chopped
- 1 tbsp red wine vinegar
- 120g walnuts, chopped

1 Heat the oil in a large pan over a medium heat. Fry the aubergine, in batches, for 5 minutes, until it starts to turn golden. Transfer to a plate.
2 Fry the onion, garlic, parsley and paprika for 5 minutes. Stir in the aubergine and tomato, and season. Add the vinegar and 200ml of water (or enough to cover).
3 Simmer gently, stirring from time to time, for 30 minutes or until tender and thickened.
4 Add the nuts and cook for 10 minutes. Serve warm or cold.
Per serving 307 cals, 27.8g fat (3.6g sat fats), 5.7g protein, 9.4g carbs, 8g sugars

PAPAYA SALAD

Serves 6 (DF) (GF)

- 2 green papaya, peeled and sliced
- 2 carrots, peeled and shredded
- 100g peanuts, roasted and crushed
- 300g small tomatoes, sliced
- 1 red chilli, sliced

Dressing

- 4 tsp fish sauce
- 2 garlic cloves, peeled and crushed
- 2 tsp soft light brown sugar
- Juice of 2 limes

1 Combine all the dressing ingredients in a bowl and stir until the sugar has dissolved.
2 Toss all of the salad ingredients through the dressing, then serve immediately.
Per serving 137 cals, 8.6g fat (1.6g sat fats), 5.4g protein, 10g carbs, 6.6g sugars

PAPAYA SALAD

FROM TOP:
PEA, BROAD BEAN,
PISTACHIO & HERB SALAD;
HARISSA-SPICED ROASTED
CAULIFLOWER, POTATO &
CHICKPEAS; GRATED RAW
CARROT SALAD WITH PINE
NUTS & BARBERRIES

Fresh veggies are full of flavour, so when cooking them you want to retain all that great taste. Pop your veg in a pan with just a little boiling water, then cover tightly with a lid to keep in the steam – this makes for quicker cooking and helps avoid soggy, overcooked greens. (You could also use a steamer or microwave.) Don't throw away the cooking liquid once the veg is done – in many cases, it can be used in soups or sauces. You'll not only get back some the lost vitamins and nutrients, but bring a bit of that great flavour to whatever you're adding it to!

PEA, BROAD BEAN, PISTACHIO & HERB SALAD
Serves 6 (DF)(GF)(V)(VG)

- 200g fresh peas
- 200g broad beans, podded, skins removed from big beans
- 100g purslane leaves or watercress (see note)
- 100g rocket
- 20g dill fronds
- 25g edible flowers (see note)
- 50g pistachios, chopped

Dressing
- Zest and juice of ½ lemon
- 4 tbsp extra-virgin olive oil
- 1 tbsp white balsamic vinegar (see note)

1 Bring a large pan of water to the boil and cook the peas and beans for 2 minutes. Refresh under cold water and leave to drain in a colander.
2 Toss all the leaves and herbs in a bowl, scatter with the beans, peas, flowers and pistachios.
3 When you're ready to eat, shake the dressing ingredients in a jar and drizzle over the salad.
Note You can buy purslane from herbsunlimited.co.uk and edible flowers from firstleaf.co.uk. White balsamic vinegar is less syrupy and sweet than the black stuff and is available in supermarkets.
Per serving 183 cals, 13.5g fat (2g sat fats), 7.2g protein, 8.3g carbs, 2.5g sugars

HARISSA-SPICED ROASTED CAULIFLOWER, POTATO & CHICKPEAS
Serves 6 (DF)(GF)(V)(VG)

- 1 large cauliflower, broken into florets
- 450g new potatoes, halved and parboiled
- 3 tbsp rose harissa
- 1 tsp ground cumin
- 1 tsp ground coriander
- 1 tbsp olive oil
- 400g tin chickpeas, drained
- 1 red onion, finely sliced
- Zest and juice of 1 lemon
- 25g parsley, roughly chopped

1 Preheat the oven to 220C/gas 7. Toss the cauliflower with the potatoes and harissa, spices, olive oil and chickpeas, then tip into a roasting tin. Roast for 30 minutes or until the cauliflower is tender.
2 Tip into a serving dish, then scatter with the onion, lemon juice and zest, and parsley to serve.
Per serving 184 cals, 4.3g fat (0.6g sat fats), 9.8g protein, 27.4g carbs, 5.3g sugars

GRATED RAW CARROT SALAD WITH PINE NUTS & BARBERRIES
Serves 6 (DF)(GF)(V)(VG)

- 50g dried barberries or sour cherries (see note)
- 1 tbsp gram flour (chickpea flour)
- 500g carrots, grated
- 50g pine nuts, toasted
- 1 bunch of mint, leaves picked and roughly torn
- 1 bunch of coriander, leaves picked and roughly torn
- 4 spring onions, finely sliced

Dressing
- Zest and juice of 1 lemon
- 2 tbsp extra-virgin olive oil

1 Soak the berries or cherries in cold water for 20 minutes to soften.
2 Meanwhile, heat a small frying pan and toast the flour until dark golden and fragrant. Leave to cool.
3 Put all the salad ingredients in a large bowl and toss.
4 Whisk the dressing ingredients, season and pour over the salad.
Note Dried barberries, from Iran, add an intense colour and tart flavour. You can buy them at ottolenghi.co.uk.
Per serving 161 cals, 10.3g fat (1.1g sat fats), 2.9g protein, 14.6g carbs, 12.3g sugars

ROASTED BROCCOLI & CAULIFLOWER WITH GARLIC & LEMON

Serves 4

- 1 head of broccoli, broken into small florets
- 1 large head of cauliflower, broken into small florets
- 4 garlic cloves, sliced thinly
- 2 lemons, thinly sliced
- 3 tbsp olive oil

1 Preheat the oven to 220C/gas 7. Mix all of the ingredients in a large bowl until everything is coated in the oil, then tip out onto a baking tray (you may need two).
2 Place in the oven to bake for 25–30 minutes, tossing the vegetables halfway through, until brown and tender.
3 Remove from the oven and serve immediately.

For more great ways to prepare fresh veggies, go to loveyourgreens.co.uk

PARSNIP & CHESTNUT TARTE TATIN

PARSNIP & CHESTNUT TARTE TATIN

Serves 6-8

- 20g goose fat
- 50g butter
- 2 parsnips, halved
- 3 shallots, peeled and halved
- 100g ready-to-cook chestnuts
- 7 sprigs of thyme
- 320g ready-rolled puff pastry
- ½ bramley apple, finely chopped
- 1 tbsp balsamic vinegar

Shallot compote
- ½ tbsp olive oil
- 200g shallots, peeled and thinly sliced
- 1 tbsp dijon mustard
- ½ tbsp balsamic vinegar
- ½ tbsp honey
- ½ tbsp dark brown sugar
- 50g medjool dates, finely chopped

1 To make the compote, add the oil to a medium pan over a low-medium heat. Add the shallots and cook for 5 minutes, until tender. Stir in the mustard, balsamic, honey, sugar, dates and 115ml of water. Season well and reduce the heat to low.
2 Cook for 10-15 minutes, stirring occasionally, until the shallots have

caramelised and the mixture has thickened. Take off the heat and let it cool while you make the pastry.
3 Preheat the oven to 200C/gas 6. Heat the goose fat and butter in a 22cm-wide ovenproof frying pan over a low-medium heat. Add the parsnips and shallots, cut-side down, and cook for 10 minutes, until they begin to caramelise.
4 Add the chestnuts and thyme sprigs, season well and cook for 5 minutes. Remove from the heat and top with about half of the shallot compote.
5 Roll out the pastry and trim it so it's slightly bigger than your pan. Remove the pan from the heat and roll the pastry over the top, tucking around the edges. Bake for about 30 minutes, until the pastry is golden and crisp on top.
6 Meanwhile, place the apple in a pan with 100ml of water. Simmer over a medium heat for 10 minutes, until soft. Season and add the balsamic.
7 Serve the tarte tatin hot with the apple balsamic sauce on the side.
Per serving 386 cals, 24.6g fat (11.7g sat fats), 5g protein, 47.1g carbs, 9.9g sugars

GARDEN HARVEST SALAD & STRAWBERRY DRESSING
(Pictured on p57)
Use all the young new growth of seasonal vegetables. Anything budding that is edible - flowers, herbs, leaves, and so on.
Serves 4 (DF) (GF) (V) (VG)
- 2 garlic cloves, peeled
- 200g strawberries (about 5-6 large berries)
- 6 tbsp extra-virgin olive oil
- 2 tbsp balsamic vinegar
- 200g mixed salad leaves
- 100g soft herbs (such as chervil, basil, mint, oregano, bay leaves)

1 Finely grate the garlic cloves into a bowl, then coarsely grate over the strawberries. Add the olive oil and balsamic, and season well.

2 Combine the salad leaves and herbs in a serving bowl, then serve with the dressing on the side.
Per serving 208 cals, 18.4g fat (2.6g sat fats), 1.9g protein, 8.7g carbs, 6.7g sugars

CHERRY & LENTIL SALAD
Serves 4 (GF) (V)
(Not pictured)
- 250g puy lentils
- 350g mixed cherries, half of them halved and stoned, the rest left whole
- 1 tbsp sherry vinegar
- Extra-virgin olive oil
- 50g whole almonds
- Juice of 1 lemon
- 50g baby spinach
- 50g feta cheese

1 Preheat the oven to 200C/gas 6. Cook the lentils according to the packet instructions, then drain. Set aside until they have cooled slightly.
2 Meanwhile, put the cherries in a large roasting tray along with the sherry vinegar, a drizzle of olive oil and a good pinch of salt and pepper. Toss so that all the cherries are thoroughly coated. Place the tray in the oven for 10-12 minutes, or until the cherries are sticky and slightly softened.
3 Put a small frying pan over a high heat and toast the almonds for 1-2 minutes, until golden. Tip into a pestle and mortar and lightly crush.
4 Once the cherries are cooked, spoon them onto a serving dish or platter. Add the lemon juice to the roasting tray, along with three times as much olive oil and season to taste. Stir well with a wooden spoon, scraping any sticky bits from the bottom of the tray.
5 Pour the dressing over the cherries, add the spinach and lentils and toss everything together. To serve, crumble over the feta and sprinkle with the almonds.
Per serving 407 cals, 19.9g fat (4.1g sat fats), 18.3g protein, 41g carbs, 11.3g sugars

CAULIFLOWER CREME BRULEE
Some veg, such as mild, creamy cauliflower, can be used in sweet dishes – such as this clever dessert.
Serves 12
- 12 egg yolks
- 220g caster sugar
- 200g cauliflower florets, finely sliced
- 1 litre greek yoghurt
- 1 tbsp vanilla extract
- 50g brown sugar

1 Combine the yoghurt, vanilla and cauliflower in a pan. Bring to boil, then simmer until the cauliflower is tender.
2 Blend in a food processor, and then pass through a sieve.
3 Whisk the egg yolks and sugar. Add the yoghurt to the egg mix and pour into 12 ramekins.
4 Sit the ramekins in a shallow pan of water in the oven at 110C/gas ¼ for 60 minutes, or until the mixture has set.
5 Leave to cool, then sprinkle with brown sugar and caramelise with a torch or grill before serving.

EST.1963

Enjoy flavours from across the globe with our range of herbs, spices, blends and pastes made using the finest ingredients.

To share your recipes and taste sensations use #BartSensation

For recipes and to see our full range
www.bart-ingredients.co.uk

Discover a
TASTE
·SENSATION·

FISH & SEAFOOD

BART®

SALT-BAKED SEA TROUT
WITH ALMOND & BROAD BEAN SALAD

SALT-BAKED SEA TROUT WITH ALMOND & BROAD BEAN SALAD

Baking a whole trout in salt prevents it drying out. It's fun to take it to the table in its crust and break it open in front of everyone.

Serves 6-8 (DF) (GF)

- 1 lemon
- A handful of soft herb sprigs, (dill or fennel fronds, parsley, chervil)
- 1 large sea trout (2.5kg), gutted and scaled, head and tail left on
- 3kg coarse rock salt
- 4 egg whites
- 2 eggs
- 4 rosemary sprigs, leaves picked and chopped

Almond & broad bean salad

- 75g whole blanched almonds
- 300g broad beans, podded
- Finely chopped flesh of 2 small preserved lemons
- 500g baby spinach
- 3 tbsp extra-virgin olive oil
- Small handful of dill, finely chopped

1 Preheat the oven to 200C/gas 6. Zest the lemon, slice it into rounds and tuck them and the herb sprigs into the belly of the trout.
2 Combine the rock salt, egg whites, eggs, rosemary and lemon zest with three tablespoonfuls of water. Lay half the mixture in a roasting tin that's big enough to fit the fish snugly. Nestle the fish in the salt bed and pat the rest of it on top (head and tail exposed). Bake for 55 minutes, until a hard crust forms.
3 Spread the almonds in a roasting pan and toast in the oven for 6 minutes, or until golden brown. Remove and set aside to cool.
4 Put the broad beans in a pan, cover with boiling water and simmer for 2 minutes. Refresh under cold water in a colander to cool slightly and remove their dull green skins. Mix with the chopped preserved lemons, spinach, almonds, olive oil and dill. Season with pepper, but not salt.
5 To check the fish is cooked, insert a skewer through the crust for a few seconds - it should come out hot to

SALMON DEVILLED EGGS

the touch. Crack and remove the crust, brush away any visible salt, then carefully fillet the fish and serve with the salad.
Per serving 493 cals, 24.7g fat (1.5g sat fats), 61.8g protein, 6.1g carbs, 2.7g sugars

SALMON DEVILLED EGGS

Makes 16 (DF)

- 8 eggs
- 25g smoked salmon, finely chopped
- 2 tsp finely chopped dill, plus extra for serving
- A pinch of cayenne pepper

Mayonnaise

- 1 egg yolk
- 2 tsp dijon mustard
- 20ml lemon juice
- 100ml olive oil
- 100ml sunflower oil

1 In a saucepan, cover the eggs with cold water and bring to the boil over a high heat. Simmer for 6 minutes, then drain and pop the eggs in cold water to cool. Peel and halve them lengthways, scoop the yolks into a bowl and roughly mash. Set aside.
2 Make your mayonnaise. In a bowl, whisk the egg yolk, mustard and lemon juice with an electric whisk until frothy. Combine the oils in a jug, then drizzle them into the egg mixture, whisking constantly until combined. Season to taste.
3 Add 60g of mayo to the egg yolks (the rest will keep in the fridge for a few days). Stir in the salmon, dill and cayenne, then mash to combine. Spoon into the egg whites, top with the extra dill and serve immediately.
Per serving 73 cals, 6.4g fat (1.3g sat fats), 4g protein, 0.1g carbs, 0g sugars

CURRIED LENTIL FISHCAKES

BESUGO AL HORNO
(Baked sea bream with potatoes)
You can try any type of sea bream, or even sea bass, in this simple and much loved Spanish recipe.
Serves 4 (DF)

- 1.5kg potatoes, peeled and thinly sliced
- 3 tbsp mixed herbs, such as flat-leaf parsley, thyme, rosemary and marjoram, all finely chopped
- 4 fresh bay leaves
- 6 tbsp olive oil, plus extra for drizzling
- 1½ tbsp smoked paprika
- 80g fresh breadcrumbs
- 2 garlic cloves, peeled and finely chopped
- 2 sea bream (about 450g each), cleaned
- 1 lemon, halved lengthways and cut into 6 wedges
- Green salad, to serve

1 Preheat your oven to 200C/gas 6. Put the potato slices in a large bowl with half the mixed herbs, the bay leaves, olive oil and ½ tablespoon of the smoked paprika, then mix well.
2 Combine the breadcrumbs, garlic, the rest of the herbs and remaining paprika in a bowl. Set aside.
3 Make three thick slashes across the sides of each fish. Insert a wedge of lemon, skin-side up, in each cut. Spread the potato mixture in an even layer in the bottom of a metal baking dish, large enough to accommodate the two sea bream. Season well, then lay the fish side by side on top of the potatoes.
4 Sprinkle the breadcrumb mixture over the top of the fish, then drizzle with the extra olive oil. Pour about 100ml of water into the bottom of the baking dish, then bake in the oven for 30–40 minutes, or until the sea bream is flaky and the potatoes are cooked. Serve immediately with a green salad.

Per serving 758 cals, 28.5g fat (3g sat fats), 54g protein, 76.5g carbs, 3g sugars

CURRIED LENTIL FISHCAKES
Serves 4 (DF)

- 200g dried yellow or red lentils
- A bunch of coriander, leaves picked, stalks finely chopped
- 1 tsp curry powder
- ½ tsp garam masala
- 1 tsp finely grated ginger
- 1 red chilli, finely chopped
- 350g undyed smoked haddock, cut into chunks
- Olive oil
- Mango chutney, grated carrot and orange segments, to serve

1 Wash the lentils, then cover with cold water, pop a lid on and gently simmer for 20–30 minutes or until soft and slightly mushy.
2 Meanwhile, put the coriander stalks in a bowl, along with the spices, chilli, half the fish and the seasoning. When the lentils are ready, drain and allow to cool.
3 Blitz half the lentils and the remaining fish in a food processor until just coming together. Add to the spice and fish mix, along with the rest of the lentils. With your hands, mix well, then form eight cakes – make sure they're firm, or they may break in the pan. Chill for 30 minutes.
4 Add a glug of olive oil to a non-stick pan over a medium-high heat. Fry the fishcakes for 4 minutes on each side, until brown and crisp on the outside and cooked through.
5 Serve with a dollop of mango chutney and a salad of carrot, orange segments and remaining coriander leaves, dressed with olive oil.

Per serving 259 cals, 3.9g fat (0.5g sat fats), 29g protein, 29g carbs, 1.5g sugars

BESUGO AL HORNO

JAMIE'S CHILLI CRAB

JAMIE'S CHILLI CRAB

This is a real treat – and one best eaten with your hands!

Serves 4–6 ⓓⒻ

- 1 large cooked crab (1.2kg)
- 1 large bunch of coriander, leaves picked, stalks finely chopped
- 4 spring onions, whites finely chopped and greens finely sliced into matchsticks
- Groundnut oil
- 1 garlic clove, peeled and finely chopped
- A thumb-sized piece of ginger, finely grated
- 1 red chilli, deseeded and finely chopped, plus extra to serve
- ½ tsp cornflour
- Roti, to serve

Chilli sauce
- 1 onion, peeled and chopped
- 2 garlic cloves, peeled and chopped
- 3 red chillies, chopped
- 2 sticks of lemongrass, bashed, peeled and chopped
- 1 tbsp white wine vinegar
- 1 tsp dark brown soft sugar
- 1 heaped tbsp tomato purée
- 1 tbsp sweet chilli sauce
- 1 tsp shrimp paste

MOROCCAN-STYLE BRAISED FISH

1 To prepare the crab, twist off the legs and claws. Turn the crab upside down, hold both sides and, with your thumbs, push under the central body until it breaks away. Remove and discard the spongy gills and carefully pick out any white meat. Scoop out the brown meat from the main shell and place in a bowl. Crack the large claws in half and pick out the meat. Reserve the legs, claws and meat and discard the other bits of the crab.
2 Place coriander leaves and spring onion greens in a bowl of iced water.
3 Next, make your chilli sauce. Add all the ingredients to a food processor, with the remaining coriander stalks, and blitz until finely chopped. Place a frying pan over a medium heat, add this paste and cook for 8–10 minutes, until coloured.
4 Place a wok over a medium heat along with a little oil. Once hot, add the chopped white spring onion,

garlic, ginger and chilli and fry for 1–2 minutes, until cooked through.
5 Add the crab legs and claws. Mix in the sauce paste and the cornflour diluted with 100ml of warm water, bring it to the boil, simmer for 5 minutes, then take off the heat, season, and add the crabmeat.
6 Serve with the drained coriander leaves and spring onions, red chilli and roti for dipping into the sauce.
Per serving 202 cals, 7.3g fat (0.8g sat fats), 22.9g protein, 11.2g carbs, 7.5g sugars

....

MOROCCAN-STYLE BRAISED FISH

If you don't have saffron, a tiny pinch of turmeric will do.

Serves 4 ⓓⒻ ⒼⒻ
- 1 litre hot fish stock
- A large pinch of saffron threads

- 400g tinned chickpeas, drained and rinsed
- 2 tbsp ras el hanout
- 600g skinless cod or haddock fillets, cut into chunks
- 4 spring onions, finely sliced
- 1 tbsp rose harissa paste
- 4 large ripe tomatoes, deseeded and chopped
- 4 tbsp chopped coriander

1 Put the fish stock, saffron and chickpeas in a large pan. Bring to the boil and simmer for 1–2 minutes.
2 Coat the fish in the ras el hanout. Stir the spring onion and harissa into the stock pan. Add the fish and poach over a low heat for 3–5 minutes.
3 Stir in the tomato and coriander and heat for 1 minute, then serve.
Per serving 282 cals, 5g fat (0.7g sat fats), 37.5g protein, 20.9g carbs, 5g sugars

ESPETO DE SARDINAS

ESPETO DE SARDINAS
(Barbecued sardines)
This technique of barbecuing whole, skewered sardines over an open fire comes from Malaga, in Andalusia. If using wooden skewers, soak them first.
Serves 4-8 (DF) (GF)
- 8 small sardines
- Olive oil
- Rock salt
- Lemon wedges, to serve

1 Make an incision in the lower part of the belly of each sardine and hook out the innards with your finger. Rinse the fish under cold running water, then dry thoroughly with kitchen paper. Alternatively, you can ask your fishmonger to do this.
2 Preheat a barbecue or griddle to full whack. Lay out as many sardines as each skewer will hold, all facing the same direction, and spear them together, from the belly up.
3 Drizzle a little olive oil and sprinkle a pinch of rock salt over both sides of the sardines. Grill them on the barbecue or griddle for 3 minutes on each side, until cooked through. Serve with a wedge of lemon.
Per serving 346 cals, 20g fat (5.7g sat fats), 41.2g protein, 0g carbs, 0g sugars

....

PLAICE GOUJONS WITH TARRAGON MUSHY PEAS & CHEAT'S CHIPS
Serves 4
- 4 tbsp plain flour
- 2 eggs, beaten
- 200g fresh breadcrumbs
- 1 tsp chilli flakes
- 4 plaice fillets
- Vegetable oil, for frying
- 1-2 cubes of bread, to test the oil
- Salad cress, to serve
Chips
- 1kg maris piper potatoes, unpeeled, cut into thin chips
- 2-3 sprigs of rosemary, leaves picked
- Olive oil
- 2 garlic cloves, peeled and finely sliced
Mushy peas
- A large knob of butter
- 400g fresh peas
- A small bunch of tarragon, leaves picked and finely chopped
- A squeeze of lemon juice, plus lemon wedges to serve

1 Preheat the oven to 200C/gas 6. For the chips, parboil the potatoes in a pan of boiling salted water for 2-3 minutes, then drain and steam-dry.
2 Place on a baking tray and toss with the rosemary, a good glug of oil and a pinch of salt. Bake for 20 minutes, then give them a good stir. Add the garlic and continue cooking for 15-20 minutes, until crisp.
3 Meanwhile, for the mushy peas, melt the butter in a medium pan over a medium heat, then add the peas and tarragon. Cook, covered, for 10-12 minutes, until they are soft.
4 Add the lemon juice and season. Mash until mushy, then keep warm.
5 Put the flour, egg and breadcrumbs on three separate plates. Season the crumbs with the chilli flakes, salt and pepper. Dust each fillet in the flour, then dip in the beaten egg, shaking off any excess, and finally coat with the chilli breadcrumbs. Season, set aside and repeat with all the fillets.
6 Heat 2cm of oil in a deep frying pan over a medium heat until shimmering – a cube of bread should turn golden in 30 seconds when dropped in.
7 Add the fish, in batches, and cook for 2-3 minutes each side. Remove with a fish slice and drain on kitchen paper. Slice each fillet into three and serve with the mushy peas, chips, lemon wedges and cress.
Per serving 707 cals, 19.9g fat (5g sat fats), 42.2g protein, 96.4g carbs, 5.6g sugars

PLAICE GOUJONS WITH TARRAGON
MUSHY PEAS & CHEAT'S CHIPS

STEAMED SEA BASS

This is often served for Chinese New Year – the fish is cooked twice and served whole to represent togetherness and good fortune.

Serves 4 (DF) (GF)

- Vegetable oil
- 2 x 5mm slices of ginger
- 1 x 600–800g whole sea bass scaled and gutted (ask your fishmonger to do this for you)
- 2 spring onions, chopped, to serve

Sauce

- 100g minced pork or chicken breast
- 3 garlic cloves, peeled and minced
- A large chunk of ginger, peeled, crushed, then chopped
- 4 tbsp doubanjiang (see note)
- 4 water chestnuts, sliced
- 4 tbsp red chilli sauce
- 4 tbsp shaoxing rice wine
- 175ml chicken stock
- 1 tbsp sugar, plus extra if needed
- 1 tsp cornflour (optional)

1 Heat a good glug of oil in a large wok over a high heat. When it's nearly smoking, add the ginger slices and fry for 3 minutes to release their flavour (don't worry if they look a bit burnt). Remove and discard the ginger, leaving the oil in the pan.
2 Pat the sea bass dry with kitchen towel. Add to the pan and gently fry on one side until lightly coloured and starting to crisp. Flip and cook the other side for 2 minutes – you want to seal the fish. Once it's golden on both sides, remove from the heat, transfer to a plate and keep warm.
3 For the sauce, return the wok to a high heat, add a splash of oil, followed by the minced pork or chicken, then the garlic and ginger. Cook, stirring, for 5 minutes, until browned. Add the rest of the ingredients except for the cornflour, cook for 1 minute, then reduce the heat to a low simmer.
4 Gently return the fish to the wok and spoon over the sauce to baste it. Pop the lid on the wok and let it simmer away for 20 minutes, returning to baste the fish every 5 minutes. Taste and season, adding

more sugar if you like, and thicken with a little cornflour mixed with a small amount of water if needed.
5 Once the fish is white and flakes easily, gently transfer it to a serving plate and ladle over the sauce. Garnish with spring onions and serve.
Note Doubanjiang is a chilli paste made from broad beans. Find it at Chinese supermarkets or buy the Pixian brand at souschef.co.uk.
Per serving 335 cals, 14.3g fat (2.1g sat fats), 38.9g protein, 12.7g carbs, 9.3g sugars

....

GRILLED SARDINES ON TOAST

Serves 4 (DF)

- 2 plum tomatoes, deseeded and finely chopped
- ½ red onion, peeled and finely chopped

GRILLED SARDINES ON TOAST

- 2 tbsp chopped dill, plus extra sprigs to garnish
- 1 tbsp olive oil
- 2 tsp cider vinegar
- 4 whole sardines, butterflied into 8 fillets
- 4 thick slices of wholemeal toast
- 1 tbsp small capers

1 Preheat the grill to high. Make a salsa by combining the tomato, onion, dill, oil and vinegar in a bowl, then season.
2 Lay the fish skin-side up on a foil-lined baking tray. Season, then grill, without turning, for 2–3 minutes, until the flesh is opaque and flaky.
3 Top each toast slice with two fish fillets, a spoonful of salsa and some capers. Garnish with dill and serve.
Per serving 317 cals, 13.9g fat (3.4g sat fats), 26g protein, 23.4g carbs, 3.5g sugars

GRILLED CURRIED MACKEREL
WITH SPICED CARROT MASH

GRILLED CURRIED MACKEREL WITH SPICED CARROT MASH

Serves 4

- 4 mackerel fillets
- 800g carrots, peeled and cut into 2cm pieces
- 1 tbsp sunflower oil
- 1 tsp cumin seeds
- 3 tbsp mild curry paste
- ½ cucumber, coarsely grated
- 8 tbsp low-fat greek-style yoghurt
- Juice of 1 lime, plus lime wedges (optional) to serve
- A handful of coriander, chopped
- Watercress, to serve (optional)

1 Preheat the oven to 200C/gas 6. Make 4–5 diagonal slashes with a knife on the skin of each fish fillet. Toss the carrots with the oil and cumin, then season and spread on a foil-lined baking tray. Roast for 40 minutes, until golden.
2 Meanwhile, rub the fish flesh (but not the skin) with the paste then place on a grill rack, skin-side up.
3 Squeeze the grated cucumber to get rid of any excess water, then mix with the yoghurt and lime juice, and season. Remove the carrots from the oven and turn the grill to high. Grill the fish, without turning, for 4–5 minutes, until just cooked through.
4 Crush the carrots with a fork, mix in the coriander and divide between four plates. Top with the mackerel and serve with the yoghurt mixture, and, if desired, lime wedges and a scattering of watercress.
Per serving 477 cals, 31g fat (5.5g sat fats), 34.9g protein, 15.5g carbs, 14.1g sugars

LEMON SOLE SKEWERS

This sweet, delicate flatfish is ideal for these decorative rolls.
Serves 2 (DF) (GF)

- 4 lemon sole fillets, skinned and pin-boned
- 4 jarred roasted red peppers in oil, drained, sliced along one side and opened out like a book
- 4 tiny pinches of saffron
- 2 long, woody rosemary stalks
- Olive oil
- Green salad, to serve

Herb salsa

- 6 green olives, chopped
- A small handful of parsley, leaves picked and chopped
- A squeeze of lemon juice
- 2 tbsp olive oil

1 Preheat the oven to 200C/gas 6. Lay the sole fillets out on a chopping board. Place a red pepper over each one. Sprinkle a tiny pinch of saffron on each, along with a good pinch of salt and pepper.
2 Roll each fillet up tightly and place in a row with a little space between each. Pull the leaves off the rosemary stalks, leaving just a few at one end.
3 Poke one stalk just left of centre through all the rolls, to hold them together. Repeat with the other stalk, just right of centre. Slice straight down through the centre, to give you eight mini rolls.
4 Lightly grease a baking tray with olive oil and lay the skewers out on them. Drizzle with a little more oil and place in the oven. Roast the skewers for 6 minutes, or until just the fish is cooked through.
5 Meanwhile, make your herb salsa by combining all of the ingredients in a bowl, then season to taste with salt and pepper.
6 Dress the cooked skewers with the salsa and serve with a green salad.
Per serving 365 cals, 16.9g fat (2.5g sat fats), 46.7g protein, 6.2g carbs, 5.3g sugars

LEMON SOLE SKEWERS

From sole to salmon, mussels to prawns, to get the best out of your seafood all you really need is the simple addition of herbs and spices. Bart Ingredients has a whole range to rev up your fish dishes, be it saffron for your paella, parsley for a fish pie, zingy lemon pepper to complement your cod, tarragon to add a sweet aniseed twist to monkfish, or cumin and turmeric for your Goan curry. From the everyday to the exotic, the possibilities are endless – it's all about bringing together simple ingredients to create loads of flavour

ARTICHOKES ALLA ROMANA

ARTICHOKES ALLA ROMANA

This dish is a staple of Roman trattorie. We've added lovely lemon sole to this classic recipe.

Serves 4 (DF)

- 16 baby globe artichokes
- 1 lemon, zested and cut into wedges
- 100ml olive oil
- 3 bay leaves
- 150ml white wine
- 4 double lemon sole fillets, skinned and pin-boned
- ½ small bunch each of mint and flat-leaf parsley

Stuffing

- 30g fresh breadcrumbs
- 25g mint, finely chopped
- 25g flat-leaf parsley, finely chopped
- 3 garlic cloves, peeled and finely chopped
- 2 tbsp extra-virgin olive oil
- 1 tsp small capers, finely chopped
- 3 anchovies in olive oil, drained and finely chopped

1 Prepare the artichokes by peeling off and discarding a few of the outer petals, until you reach the pale, tender centre. Trim the top and stem end with a knife or scissors. Remove the inedible choke using a small paring knife or teaspoon. Put the artichokes in a bowl of cold water with the juice of one of the lemon wedges to stop them browning.
2 To make the stuffing, combine all the ingredients together in a bowl and season well with black pepper. Spoon the stuffing into the cavity of each artichoke.
3 Pour the olive oil into a pan that's large enough for all the artichokes to fit snugly. Arrange them in the pan so they are all touching one another and remain upright. Scatter any leftover stuffing over the top, then tuck the bay leaves and remaining lemon wedges into the pan.
4 Pour the white wine and enough boiling water into the pan to come a third of the way up the sides of the artichokes, then bring to the boil.

FREGOLA AND MUSSEL STEW

5 Reduce the temperature, then make a cartouche with a circle of greaseproof paper. Dampen it under running water and place on top of the artichokes, underneath the lid.
6 Simmer for about 30 minutes, until the water has evaporated and the bottoms of the artichokes are beginning to brown and caramelise. Test them with a small sharp knife to ensure they are tender.
7 Season the sole fillets and scatter lemon zest over each one. Gently fold each one over and place them on top of the artichokes, under the cartouche. Gently steam for 4–6 minutes, until the fish is opaque.
8 Serve with the mint and parsley, roughly chopped and scattered over the top of the dish.

Per serving 486 cals, 34g fat (4.9g sat fats), 30.8g protein, 11.5g carbs, 3.5g sugars

FREGOLA & MUSSEL STEW

Serves 4 (DF)

- 2 tbsp olive oil
- 2 garlic cloves, peeled and chopped
- 1 red chilli, finely chopped
- 400g mussels in their shells
- 400ml fish stock
- 400g passata
- 100g fregola, cooked (see note)
- A small handful of parsley, to serve

1 Heat the oil in pan over a medium heat and sauté the garlic, chilli and mussels for 5 minutes. Discard any shells that don't open.
2 Add the stock and passata, cover and cook for 5–6 minutes. Stir in the pasta and top with parsley.
Note Fregola is a Sardinian pasta like couscous. Find it at etruscany.co.uk.

Per serving 212 cals, 7.9g fat (1.1g sat fats), 9.5g protein, 26g carbs, 6.4g sugars

SMOKED SALMON & PRAWN
COCKTAIL SALAD

HERB-CRUSTED HALIBUT WITH GHERKIN SAUCE

Serves 4

- 4 x 175g thick halibut fillets, skinned
- 4 slices of wholemeal bread, toasted, crusts removed, and chopped
- 2 garlic cloves, peeled and crushed
- Juice and grated zest of 1 lemon
- A small bunch fresh tarragon, roughly chopped
- A small bunch fresh chives, roughly chopped
- A small bunch fresh dill, roughly chopped
- 4 tbsp olive oil
- 8 tbsp light mayonnaise
- 6 tbsp plain yoghurt
- 8 gherkins, roughly chopped
- 1 tbsp small capers, drained and chopped
- Crisp green salad, to serve

1 Preheat the oven to 230C/gas 8. Line a baking sheet with baking paper. Season the halibut and place, skinned-side down, on the paper.
2 Put the chopped toast in a food processor with the garlic and lemon zest and blitz it into fine crumbs. Add all the fresh herbs and pulse again, until everything is chopped and combined. Add 2 teaspoons lemon juice and half the oil, season and pulse briefly to mix.
3 Gently press the breadcrumb mixture on top of each piece of fish. Drizzle with the remaining oil and place on the top shelf of the oven for around 10–12 minutes, or until the topping is lightly golden and the fish is cooked through.
4 Meanwhile, make the sauce by combining the mayonnaise, yoghurt, gherkins, capers and a squeeze of lemon juice. Season well. Serve the fish with the gherkin sauce, a wedge of lemon and a green salad.

Per serving 519 cals, 28.8g fat (4.9g sat fats), 43.9g protein, 22.6g carbs, 5.4g sugars

SMOKED SALMON & PRAWNS COCKTAIL SALAD

Liven up this seafood medley with a spicy cocktail sauce, or opt for our mellower version.

Serves 6 (DF)

- 3 baby gem lettuces, leaves separated
- 300g smoked salmon, thinly sliced
- 24 large cooked prawns

Miami-style spiced cocktail sauce

- 4 tbsp mayonnaise
- 4 tbsp ketchup
- 2 tbsp hot chilli sauce
- 1 tsp english mustard
- 1 tsp finely grated ginger
- ½ tsp crushed garlic
- 1 spring onion, finely chopped
- 1 tbsp chopped coriander
- Lime juice and olive oil, to serve

Mellow cocktail sauce

- 4 tbsp mayonnaise
- 4 tbsp ketchup
- ½ tsp cayenne pepper
- A little lemon juice, to serve

1 Start by making your sauce. For either option, mix all the ingredients in a bowl and refrigerate for 1 hour.
2 Divide the lettuce leaves between serving plates. Drape the smoked salmon over the leaves and arrange the prawns on top.
3 Dress the salad generously with your preferred cocktail sauce. For a finishing touch, squeeze lemon juice over the mild version; for the spicy sauce, finish with lime juice, a drizzle of oil and some black pepper.

Per serving (spiced) 169 cals, 8.9g fat (1.8g sat fats), 16.8g protein, 5.2g carbs, 4.9g sugars
Per serving (mellow) 163 cals, 8.8g fat (1.8g sat fats), 16.6g protein, 4g carbs, 3.9g sugars

HERB-CRUSTED HALIBUT
WITH GHERKIN SAUCE

JOURNEY OF DISCOVERY

From the sunny shores of Portugal, across the continent of Africa, through India and Thailand, and onto South America, The Bart Ingredients Co. have sourced delicious regional ingredients to create this authentic range of fragrant blends.

Take a journey through the world's exotic spice trails in your own kitchen, with their many inspirational flavours.

They're simple to use, and add a dash of exotic character to simple ingredients. Why not try these simple hints and tips to spice up your everyday cuisines.

- Add Bart Pilau spice blend to kedgeree whilst cooking
- To give a kick to your houmous, throw in some Bart Baharat
- Mix Bart Piri Piri, lemon juice and oil with your prawns prior to cooking
- Scatter Bart Creole or Fajita spice blend into eggs before scrambling
- Melt some white chocolate, add a pinch of Bart Ras el Hanout and set into a block for a tasty after-dinner treat
- Add a Thai twist to cured salmon, in our recipe, far right

WATERCRESS PANCAKES WITH CRAB & CREME FRAÍCHE

WATERCRESS PANCAKES WITH CRAB & CREME FRAICHE
Makes 8 pancakes (serves 4)
- 100g watercress, plus extra to serve
- 175g self-raising flour
- 1 large egg, beaten
- 275ml milk
- A pinch of chilli flakes
- 1 lemon, halved (zest and juice of half, half for wedges to serve)
- 200g crabmeat, brown and white
- 1 small bunch of dill, finely chopped
- Olive oil
- 100g crème fraîche

1 Place the watercress in a food processor and blitz until smooth. Add the flour, egg, milk, chilli flakes and a pinch of salt and pepper. Grate in the zest from half a lemon and blitz to combine.
2 Season the crabmeat with a pinch of black pepper, most of the dill and a squeeze of lemon juice. Cut the remaining lemon into wedges.
3 Heat a splash of olive oil in a medium non-stick frying pan over a medium heat. To make pancakes, ladle spoonfuls of batter into the pan and cook for 3-4 minutes, flipping halfway, until all the batter is used. Tilt the pan to distribute the batter and ensure evenly cooked pancakes.
4 Serve the pancakes with the crabmeat and a spoonful of crème fraîche, sprinkled with the remaining dill, a drizzle of olive oil plus a wedge of lemon and a little watercress on the side of the plate.
Per serving 182 cals, 8.3g fat (4.3g sat fats), 9.1g protein, 18.9g carbs, 2.4g sugars

FISH TACOS WITH RHUBARB SALSA

THAI CURED SALMON
Serves 8
- 1.25kg tail piece of salmon, halved, filleted, skin left on
- 100g coarse sea salt
- 100g golden caster sugar
- 2 tbsp Bart Aromatic Thai spice blend
- Grated zest of 1 lime

Mango & cucumber relish
- 1 large mango, peeled and diced
- ¼ cucumber, deseeded and diced
- ½ red chilli, deseeded and finely chopped
- 3 spring onions, finely chopped
- Juice of 1 lime
- 1 tsp fish sauce
- 2 tbsp chopped fresh coriander

1 Check the salmon for bones by running your fingers along the flesh and then pulling out the bones using a pair of tweezers.
2 In a bowl, combine the salt, sugar and spice blend and rub some of it into the fish. Line a dish big enough to fit the salmon with 2 layers of foil.
3 Place a piece of salmon skin-side down on the foil. Spread over the spice mix then top with the other piece of salmon, skin-side up. Pull the foil over the fish then place a board and weights on top. Leave in the fridge for 2-4 days, turning now and then, pouring off any liquid.
4 An hour before serving, mix all the relish ingredients in a bowl; set aside. Take the foil off the salmon, scrape off the cure and slice thinly across the grain. Serve with the relish.

FISH TACOS WITH RHUBARB SALSA
Serves 4
- 2 tbsp olive oil
- 1 tbsp paprika
- 500g salmon and pollock, skinned and cut into 2.5cm cubes
- 8 taco shells
- Iceberg lettuce, spring onions and grated cheddar, to serve

Salsa
- 150g rhubarb, diced
- ½ red pepper, deseeded and diced
- ½ red onion, peeled and diced
- ½ cucumber, diced
- Juice of 2 limes
- 1 tbsp brown muscovado sugar
- ½ tsp smoked paprika
- 2 tbsp olive oil

1 Preheat oven to 180C/gas 4. Mix all the salsa ingredients and set aside.
2 In a bowl, mix the oil and paprika, season, then toss the fish through to coat. Place on a baking sheet and cook for 10 minutes, until opaque and easily flaked.
3 Warm the taco shells in the oven, then serve with the salsa, fish, lettuce, spring onions and cheese.
Per serving 497 cals, 32.2g fat (6.4g sat fats), 28g protein, 24g carbs, 6.7g sugars

Treat yourself to something special

Enjoy the real flavour of India with my delicious range of authentic chutneys and curry pastes made with the finest ingredients and a whole lot of love and know-how.

Geeta Samtani

Geeta's®
The Real Flavour of India

Check out our full range and find out more at **geetasfoods.com**

Available at most leading supermarkets

POULTRY

Geeta's
The Real Flavour of India

POACHED CHICKEN
WITH PUY LENTILS

POACHED CHICKEN WITH PUY LENTILS

Serves 4 (DF) (GF)

To cut a corner, you could use ready-to-eat lentils and blanch the beans separately

- 4 skinless chicken breast fillets
- 800ml chicken stock
- 200g dried puy lentils
- 200g green beans, cut into 2cm lengths
- 2 tbsp dijon mustard
- 2 tbsp capers
- 25g flat-leaf parsley, chopped, plus extra to garnish
- 200g jar chargrilled artichokes in olive oil, drained and chopped
- 290g jar chargrilled red peppers, drained and chopped
- 2 tbsp lemon-infused olive oil

1 Put the chicken in a large pan and pour the stock over it. Bring to a boil, reduce to a medium heat, then cover and poach for 20–25 minutes, or until the meat is cooked through. Drain and keep warm.
2 Meanwhile, put the lentils in a pan and cover with cold water. Bring to the boil, reduce to a simmer and cook for 25–30 minutes, or until tender. Season, and add the beans for the last minute.
3 Drain, then stir in the mustard, capers, parsley, artichokes and peppers. Divide between warm plates, slice each chicken breast and place on top. Drizzle over the oil and garnish with the extra parsley.

Per serving 520 cals, 21.8g fat (3.1g sat fats), 43.5g protein, 30.2g carbs, 4.6g sugars

....

THE HIX TURKEY BURGER

"The best cuts of turkey to use here are the thighs, as they don't dry out during cooking," advises London restaurateur Mark Hix.
Serves 4

- 450g coarsely minced turkey thighs (you could ask your butcher to do this)
- 100g cumberland sausage meat
- 5-10 brussels sprouts, trimmed, halved and finely shredded
- 2-3 tbsp mayonnaise

THE HIX TURKEY BURGER

- Vegetable oil, for brushing
- 4 hamburger buns

Cranberry sauce
- 500g fresh or frozen cranberries
- 400ml fresh orange juice
- 250g sugar
- ½ tsp ground cinnamon
- ½ tsp ground cloves
- 1 bay leaf

1 For the sauce, put all the ingredients in a heavy-bottomed saucepan, place over a medium–high heat and bring to the boil. Lower the heat and simmer for 30 minutes, or until the cranberries have broken down a little and the liquid has thickened. Transfer to a container or sealable jar and leave to cool for about 1 hour.
2 Season the turkey, then mould it into patties a little larger than the buns. Using a 3cm circular cutter, cut a hole in the centre of each patty and pack in the sausagemeat, pressing any excess turkey meat around the edges.
3 In a bowl, combine the sprouts with enough mayonnaise to bind them, season to taste, then set aside.
4 Preheat the oven to 180C/gas 4. Brush a griddle pan with oil, place it over a medium heat and cook the burgers for 4–5 minutes on each side, until the juices run clear, then place in the oven for 5 minutes.
5 Cut the buns in half and warm them under the grill. To assemble the burgers, spread the remaining mayonnaise on the bottom of each bun, sit a burger on top, spoon on a dollop of cranberry sauce and finish with the sprouts.

Per serving 458 cals, 14.1g fat (3.8g sat fats), 31.6g protein, 51.9g carbs, 22.1g sugars

SPRING CHICKEN WITH BRAISED PEAS & GEM LETTUCE

CHARGRILLED CHICKEN WITH SWEET POTATOES & CASHEWS

Serves 4 (DF)

- 8 skinless, boneless chicken thighs
- 1½ tsp chilli flakes
- Zest of 2 lemons, juice of ½
- Olive oil
- 4 sweet potatoes (about 750g), cut into wedges
- 2 tbsp semolina
- 50g cashews
- 2 avocados, flesh only
- A handful of rocket

1 Preheat the oven to 200C/gas 6. Lay the chicken on a large sheet of greaseproof paper. Sprinkle over 1 tsp of the chilli flakes and half the zest, season and drizzle with oil.
2 Top with more paper and bash with a rolling pan until 5mm thick. Put on a plate, cover with cling film and chill.
3 Toss the sweet potato wedges with a drizzle of oil and the semolina. Roast for 25-30 minutes, tossing now and then, until golden and crispy.
4 Toast the nuts in a frying pan over a medium heat, until golden. Take off the heat, drizzle with oil and scatter with the remaining lemon zest.
5 Add the rest of the chilli and toss well. Preheat a griddle pan over a high heat. Mash the avocados in a bowl with the lemon juice and season.
6 Griddle the chicken for around 7-8 minutes, turning halfway, until cooked and golden. Slice up and serve with the sweet potatoes, avocado, rocket and cashews.

Per serving 799 cals, 42.6g fat (9.2g sat fats), 40.6g protein, 67.7g carbs, 16.4g sugars

SPRING CHICKEN WITH BRAISED PEAS & GEM LETTUCE

Serves 4

- 8 chicken thighs, skin on, bone in
- 2 sprigs of thyme
- Olive oil
- 8 spring onions, sliced
- 2 garlic cloves, peeled and sliced
- 30ml dry sherry
- 650ml hot chicken stock
- A knob of butter
- 4 little gem lettuces, halved lengthways
- 250g fresh peas (or frozen, defrosted)
- A squeeze of lemon juice
- Crusty bread, to serve

1 Rub the chicken thighs with the thyme sprigs and a glug of olive oil, and season with salt and pepper.
2 Heat a large casserole dish over a high heat and sear the chicken thighs, skin-side down, for around 5 minutes, or until the skin is lovely and golden.
3 Turn the chicken over, reduce the heat to medium, then add the spring onion and garlic. Sauté for 5 minutes, then add the dry sherry and cook for a further minute.
4 Pour the hot chicken stock into the dish, bring to a simmer, then cover and cook for about 30 minutes, until the chicken is cooked and tender.
5 Stir in the butter, baby gem lettuce and the peas, and continue to simmer for 10 minutes until soft. Add the lemon juice and season. Divide the meal between bowls, and serve with crusty bread.

Per serving 595 cals, 38.3g fat (11.9g sat fats), 49.2g protein, 12g carbs, 5.9g sugars

CRISPY DUCK WITH
CHERRY HOISIN SAUCE

CRISPY DUCK WITH CHERRY HOISIN SAUCE

Serves 6 (DF)

- 1 duck (about 1.25kg)
- 1 tsp chinese five spice
- 1 pack of chinese pancakes
- A handful of dark cherries, chopped
- 1 red chilli, thinly sliced
- ½ tbsp rice wine vinegar
- ½ tsp sugar
- 1 bunch of spring onions, finely shredded, to serve
- 1 cucumber, julienned, to serve
- ½ bunch of thai basil, to serve

Hoisin sauce

- 2 tsp sesame oil
- 1 thumb-sized piece of root ginger, peeled and finely grated
- 2 garlic cloves, peeled and minced
- A pinch of chilli flakes
- 250g dark cherries, halved and stoned
- 2 tsp rice wine vinegar
- 2 tbsp runny honey
- 1 tbsp soy sauce
- ½ tbsp black bean paste

1 Preheat the oven to its highest temperature. Half fill a large deep pan with water, place over a high heat and bring to the boil.
2 Prick the duck skin all over, then lower into the boiling water and simmer for 5 minutes.
3 Remove and place on a large plate to steam-dry for 2 minutes. Pat dry with kitchen paper, season well and rub the five spice into the skin.
4 Put the duck on a metal rack over a roasting tray and place in the oven. After 10 minutes, turn the heat down to 170C/gas 3 and roast for 1½ hours. Turn heat up again for 15 minutes until the skin is crisp.
5 To make the hoisin sauce, put the sesame oil in a small saucepan over a medium heat. Once hot, add the ginger, garlic and chilli flakes and fry for 1 minute until lightly golden.
6 Add the cherries, turn the heat down and cook for 2 minutes before adding the other ingredients and a splash of water. Turn the heat right down and simmer for 5-10 minutes, mashing the cherries from time to

CHICKEN SALAD

time until the sauce is nice and thick.
7 Remove from the heat and blitz with a stick blender until smooth. Transfer to a bowl and allow to cool.
8 Remove the duck from the oven, transfer to a board, loosely cover with foil and allow to rest for 10 minutes.
9 In a small bowl, toss together the cherries, chilli, vinegar and sugar.
10 Shred the duck and serve with warmed pancakes, hoisin sauce, spring onion, cucumber, basil and the pickled cherries with chilli.

Per serving 452 cals, 34.2g fat (9.8g sat fats), 19.5g protein, 16.7g carbs, 7.2g sugars

....

CHICKEN SALAD

Serves 4-6 (GF)

- 250g baby spinach
- 200g cooked chicken, shredded
- 50g parmesan
- 1 pomegranate, seeds only

Dressing

- 4 tsp extra-virgin olive oil
- Juice of ½ lemon
- 2 tbsp dijon mustard
- 2 tsp pomegranate molasses

1 Combine the spinach and chicken in a large salad bowl. Using a vegetable peeler, shave the cheese into wide strips and combine two-thirds with the spinach and chicken.
2 For the dressing, add all of the ingredients to a jam jar or jug and mix well. Pour over the salad and gently toss everything together.
3 Toss in the pomegranate seeds last, to avoid them sinking to the bottom, scatter over the rest of the parmesan shavings and serve.

Per serving 308 cals, 20.5g fat (4.6g sat fats), 20.5g protein, 10.2g carbs, 9g sugars

RIOJA-STYLE QUAIL

5 When you're ready to cook, preheat the oven to 190C/gas 5. Rinse the quails in cold water and pat dry.
6 Tear the peppers into big strips, removing the seeds. Sit them in a large roasting tray. Tear the bread into large croutons and scatter over the peppers. Drizzle over a little oil.
7 Put in the oven, making sure there is an oven rack shelf directly above it. Place the quail directly on the rack above the peppers and croutons.
8 Roast for 20–30 minutes, or until the quails are cooked through and tender, and the pepper has softened. Serve with the watercress.
Per serving 538 cals, 14.2g fat (3g sat fats), 45.7g protein, 61.2g carbs, 13.7g sugars

CRANBERRY & CHILLI CHICKEN WINGS
Makes 12 (DF) (GF)

- 1 large onion, peeled and finely sliced
- 4 garlic cloves, peeled and finely sliced
- 2 red chillies, deseeded and finely sliced
- Olive oil
- 200g fresh cranberries
- 4 tbsp honey
- 4 tsp red wine vinegar
- 12 chicken wings
- Chilli salt (optional)

1 Preheat the oven to 200C/gas 6. Sweat the onion, garlic and chillies in a pan with a little oil over a medium heat until caramelised.
2 Add the cranberries, honey, vinegar and a splash of water, then simmer for 10–15 minutes, until soft. Blitz in a blender until smooth, with a little oil to loosen, then season.
3 Place the wings on a baking tray, brush them all over with the berry marinade, cover with foil and bake for 25 minutes. Remove the foil, brush with more marinade and cook for 25 minutes, brushing with the marinade every so often. Sprinkle with chilli salt, if using, then serve.
Per serving 151 cals, 8.6g fat (2.2g sat fats), 13g protein, 6.2g carbs, 5.4g sugars

RIOJA-STYLE QUAIL
This is made with peppers, onions and garlic, which are all grown in the La Rioja region of Spain.
Serves 4 (DF)

- 1 tbsp cumin seeds
- 1 cinnamon stick
- 50g salt
- 50g soft light brown sugar
- 1 head of garlic
- 1 onion, peeled and cut into chunks
- 3 sprigs of rosemary, leaves picked
- ½ bunch of oregano
- 1 tsp sweet smoked paprika
- 4 pomegranates, halved
- 4 quails
- 2 large green peppers
- 2 large red peppers
- 1 large yellow pepper
- 1 loaf of artisan bread
- Extra-virgin olive oil
- Watercress, to serve

1 The night before you plan to cook, place a small frying pan over a low heat. Toast the cumin seeds and cinnamon stick until fragrant, then tip into a bowl and place to one side.
2 Prepare the brine for the quails by boiling 400ml of water in a pan. Stir in the salt, sugar and spices, until the has sugar dissolved, then turn off the heat. Add 400ml of cold water.
3 Click off the garlic cloves and gently bash with a rolling pin. Put in the pan with the onion. Add the rosemary leaves, oregano, and paprika. Squeeze the juice from the pomegranates into the pan, and stir.
4 Slash the quails' thighs, then put the birds in the brine. Cover and chill in the fridge overnight.

CRANBERRY & CHILLI
CHICKEN WINGS

MEDITERRANEAN CHICKEN TRAYBAKE

Serves 4 (DF)

- 400g cherry tomatoes, on the vine
- 1 aubergine, cut into chunks
- 2 courgettes, cut into chunks
- 2 red onions, peeled and cut into chunks
- 1 garlic bulb, cloves separated
- 1 tbsp chopped thyme leaves
- 4 tbsp olive oil
- 8 chicken thighs
- 150ml hot chicken stock
- Sourdough bread, to serve

1 Preheat the oven to 200C/gas 6. Put all the vegetables and herbs in a roasting tin, pour over the olive oil, season and toss well. Sit the chicken on top and roast for 20 minutes.
2 Turn down the oven to 180C/gas 4 and pour over the stock. Cook for 20-30 minutes, until the chicken is golden and the vegetables are tender. Squeeze the garlic cloves from their skins and mix in. Serve with chunks of sourdough bread.
Per serving 402 cals, 24.6g fat (5g sat fats), 34g protein, 12g carbs, 8.8g sugars

JERK CHICKEN

JERK CHICKEN

The key to this traditional Jamaican dish is to marinate the chicken for 24 hours, so it's imbued with all the delicious flavours. If you want to give it a bit more of a kick, just up the scotch bonnet quota.

Serves 4 (DF) (GF)

- 2kg chicken, jointed
- Rice and peas, coleslaw, barbecued corn on the cob, fried plantain and salad, to serve (optional)

Marinade (makes 250ml)

- 4 spring onions, roughly chopped
- 6 garlic cloves, peeled and roughly chopped
- 2 scotch bonnet peppers, thinly sliced
- ½ bunch of thyme, roughly chopped
- 2-3 tbsp ground allspice or ground pimento
- 2 tbsp salt
- 2 tsp ground black pepper
- 2 tbsp honey
- Juice of 1 lime
- 125ml vegetable oil

1 First, make the marinade. Put all the ingredients in a bowl and add 125ml of water. Using a hand blender, blitz everything into a thick paste.
2 Lightly score the chicken pieces with a sharp knife to allow the marinade to soak deep into the meat, then rub all over with the jerk marinade (don't use all of it – keep some for basting). Pop in the fridge for 24 hours, so the meat starts to tenderise and is infused with all the jerk flavours.
3 When you're ready to cook, grill the meat slowly – preferably on a charcoal and wood-smoke barbecue grill – for 20-25 minutes, turning every 5 minutes or so and basting with the reserved marinade sauce until the skin is crisp and golden brown in colour.
4 If you're not using a barbecue, preheat the oven to 180C/gas 4. Heat a griddle pan to medium-high and sear the chicken for 2-3 minutes on each side, until the skin begins to caramelise. Transfer the chicken to a roasting pan and cook for 25-30 minutes or until the juices run clear when a skewer is inserted.
5 Serve the chicken with rice and peas, coleslaw, barbecued corn on the cob, fried plantain and a seasonal salad – or, if you can't wait, just eat straight from the grill.
Per serving 684 cals, 46.8g fat (8g sat fats), 56g protein, 11.4g carbs, 9.8g sugars

CHICKEN MOILEE

CHICKEN MOILEE

This fragrant stew comes from the Indian state of Kerala.

Serves 4 (DF) (GF)

- 2 large green chillies, deseeded and chopped
- 2 tbsp mild or medium curry powder
- 2 tsp grated garlic
- 2 tsp grated ginger
- A large bunch of coriander, roughly chopped
- 2 tbsp vegetable oil
- 15 dried curry leaves
- 2 onions, peeled and thinly sliced
- 12 skinless chicken thigh fillets, cut into large chunks
- 200g mixed red and yellow cherry tomatoes
- 400ml coconut milk
- Juice of 1 lime
- Cucumber slices, to serve
- Cooked pilau or brown basmati rice, to serve

1 Place the chillies, curry powder, garlic, ginger and half the bunch of coriander in a food processor with a pinch of salt and 5 tablespoons water. Blend until fairly smooth.
2 Heat the vegetable oil in a large frying pan over a medium heat, then add the curry leaves and fry for around 1 minute. Now add the fresh paste and fry for 1 minute, stirring well, to cook the spices. Stir in the onion and cook over a low heat for 10 minutes.
3 Add the chicken, tomatoes, coconut milk and 200ml water and gently simmer until the chicken is cooked through, about 20 minutes. Remove from the heat, sprinkle over the remaining coriander and stir in the lime juice. Adjust the seasoning to taste, then serve with the sliced cucumber and the rice.
Per serving 425 cals, 25.2g fat (9.2g sat fats), 35.5g protein, 14.4g carbs, 10.2g sugars

CHICKEN & WILD MUSHROOM STEW

Serves 4 (GF)

- 20g butter
- 1 tbsp olive oil
- 8 skinless chicken thighs, bone in
- 1 large white onion, finely chopped
- 4 garlic cloves, sliced
- 300g mixed wild mushrooms
- 4 thyme sprigs
- 500ml white wine
- ½ large bunch of parsley, leaves picked and chopped
- Mashed potatoes and greens, to serve

1 Preheat the oven to 170C/gas 3. Put a large casserole pan over a medium heat and, once hot, add the butter and oil. Place the chicken in the pan and brown all over, about 5 minutes, then transfer to a plate to rest.
2 Add the onion and garlic to the pan and cook over a low-medium heat for 10 minutes, or until soft. Stir in the mushrooms and thyme and cook for a further 5 minutes, then return the chicken to the pan, along with the wine and a pinch of seasoning.
3 Place a cartouche of damp greaseproof paper on the top, then bake for 1 hour, or until the chicken is coming away from the bone. Sprinkle the parsley over the top and serve with the mash and greens.
Per serving 390 cals, 18.2g fat (5.8g sat fats), 31g protein, 6.2g carbs, 4g sugars

CHICKEN & WILD
MUSHROOM STEW

SLOW-COOKED
TURKEY YELLOW CURRY

SLOW-COOKED TURKEY YELLOW CURRY

This is a warming, comforting dish from Aussie chef Martin Boetz. "Yellow curry is one of my favourites in the Thai repertoire," he says. "This curry is great for entertaining because you could always make it the day before."

Serves 4 (DF)

- 60ml coconut oil or canola oil (see note)
- 2 turkey legs, skin on, each cut into 4, osso buco-style (you can ask your butcher to do this for you)
- 60g palm sugar, shaved
- 60ml fish sauce
- 400ml coconut milk
- 200ml chicken stock
- 6 kipfler or other waxy potatoes, peeled, cut into bite-sized pieces
- Steamed rice, to serve (optional)

Yellow curry paste

- 1 tsp cumin seeds
- 1 tbsp coriander seeds
- 1 tsp fennel seeds
- 2 tbsp sea salt
- ½ tsp white peppercorns
- 1 red onion, peeled and chopped
- 8 garlic cloves, peeled
- 1 tbsp galangal purée (or 4cm piece of galangal, peeled and chopped)
- 6 coriander roots, scraped, cleaned and chopped
- 4cm piece fresh turmeric, peeled and chopped
- 4cm piece fresh ginger, peeled and chopped
- 8 dried long red chillies, halved, deseeded, soaked in warm water for 20 minutes, then drained

1 Start by making your curry paste. Place the cumin, coriander and fennel seeds in a bowl, and dampen with a little cold water – this will help them cook evenly all the way through without burning. Drain and set aside.

2 Heat a heavy-based saucepan over a medium heat, add the spice seeds and toast them for 5-8 minutes, until very fragrant. Set aside to cool.
3 Once cool, add the seeds to a spice or coffee grinder with the salt and peppercorns. Grind until fine. Pass the mixture through a fine sieve.
4 In a heavy-based saucepan or wok, toast the onion, garlic, galangal, coriander roots, turmeric and ginger over a medium heat for 8-10 minutes, stirring, until coloured and softened. If the ingredients are colouring too quickly, add 50ml of water – you want them to caramelise. Scrape the mixture into a bowl, stir in the chillies and leave to cool.
5 Transfer all the ingredients to a food processor and blitz for 3-4 minutes, until you have a smooth, red-yellow paste, loosening it with up to 100ml of water if needed.
6 Heat the oil in a heavy-based saucepan over a medium heat. Add 4 tablespoons of the curry paste (keep the rest in a jar in the fridge for another time – this will keep for up to one week) and fry for 8 minutes, stirring continuously, until fragrant.
7 Add the turkey pieces to the pan and cook, stirring occasionally, for 10 minutes, or until coloured all over. Stir in the palm sugar and fish sauce and cook, stirring, until the sugar is dissolved, about 5 minutes. Pour in the coconut milk and stock. Bring it to the boil, reduce the heat to low and let it simmer for 1 hour.
8 Add the potatoes and simmer for 15-20 minutes, or until cooked and easily pierced with a skewer. Turn off the heat and let the curry rest for 15 minutes to let the flavours mingle.
9 Check the seasoning – it should be sweet, salty and aromatic. Serve the curry with steamed rice, if you like.
Note Canola is a type of rapeseed oil which contains fewer fatty acids. Buy it from amazon.co.uk or alternatively, use coconut oil.

Per serving 733 cals, 42.2g fat (19.4g sat fats), 33.2g protein, 59.5g carbs, 20.3g sugars

OREGANO CHICKEN WITH ROCKET & COURGETTE COUSCOUS

(not pictured)

Serves 4 (DF)

- 4 skinless chicken breast fillets
- Juice of 2 lemons, grated zest of 1
- 2 garlic cloves, peeled and crushed
- 1 tbsp finely chopped fresh oregano, plus extra to garnish
- 4 tbsp olive oil
- 200g couscous
- 400ml hot chicken stock
- 2 courgettes, grated
- 50g wild rocket, roughly chopped

1 Place the chicken breasts between two sheets of cling film and bash with a rolling pin until they're 1cm-thick all over.
2 In a bowl, mix the lemon zest and half of the juice, the crushed garlic, oregano and 2 tablespoons of the oil and rub this over the chicken.
3 Meanwhile, place the couscous in a large bowl and pour over the stock. Cover and leave for 5-10 minutes until all the stock has been absorbed.
4 Heat the rest of the oil in a wide frying pan and stir-fry the courgettes for 3-4 minutes, or until softened. Tip into a sieve and gently press to remove excess water. Add to the couscous and rocket, season and stir in the remaining lemon juice.
5 Heat a griddle pan over a medium-high heat and cook the chicken for 3-4 minutes on each side, pressing them onto the griddle to get even markings. You may need to do these in batches – just set aside in a warm oven until all of them are done. Serve the chicken garnished with the oregano leaves.

Per serving 403 cals, 16.8g fat (2.8g sat fats), 35.9g protein, 28.3g carbs, 2g sugars

TURKEY KOFTE

Serves 4

- 500g minced turkey
- 1 large courgette, finely grated
- 2 spring onions, finely chopped
- 1 green chilli, finely chopped
- 1 egg, lightly beaten
- 50g pistachios, chopped, a few reserved
- 3 sprigs each of coriander, parsley and mint, leaves picked and chopped
- ½ tsp dried oregano
- ¼ tsp cumin seeds, toasted

Chilli sauce

- 4 red chillies
- 4 tomatoes, halved
- 2 small onions, skin on, halved
- 4 garlic cloves, skin on, bashed
- Olive oil
- 1 tbsp brown sugar
- 2 tbsp tomato purée
- 1 tbsp red wine vinegar

Tahini yoghurt

- 250g greek yoghurt
- 1 tbsp tahini
- A squeeze of lemon juice

Turkish pilav

- Olive oil
- 1 onion, peeled and finely chopped
- 2 garlic cloves, peeled and finely chopped
- 200g bulgur wheat
- 400ml hot chicken stock
- A knob of butter
- 80g broken rice vermicelli
- 100g tinned chickpeas, drained
- Baby gem lettuce, to serve

1 To make your kofte, mix all the ingredients together in a large bowl and season well. With wet hands, form 16 kofte, each the size and shape of a small egg. Leave in the fridge to firm up for at least 30 minutes, then thread onto metal skewers, two per skewer.
2 Cook the kofte under a grill, or over a flame charcoal grill, on high for 12 minutes, until golden brown and cooked through, turning regularly.

3 Preheat the oven to 180C/gas 4. To make the chilli sauce, place the chillies, tomatoes, onions and garlic on a baking tray, drizzle with oil and roast for 25 minutes, until soft.
4 Allow to cool slightly, remove and discard the stalks from the chillies, the cores from the tomatoes and the skins from the onions and garlic. Add to a food processor, with the sugar, tomato purée and vinegar. Blitz until smooth and add a glug of oil to make it glossy. Pulse again and season.
5 For the tahini yoghurt, mix all the ingredients in a bowl and season with a pinch of salt and pepper.
6 For the pilav, add a glug of oil to a non-stick pan over a low–medium heat. Sweat the onion and garlic for 10 minutes, add the bulgur and stir to coat. Pour in the stock, bring to the boil, then reduce the heat to very low. Cover and steam for 8 minutes.
7 Meanwhile, in a separate pan, melt the butter and cook the vermicelli until the butter turns golden brown. After 8 minutes, add it to the bulgur along with the chickpeas. Don't stir at any point, just replace the lid and let it steam for another 8 minutes.
8 Turn off the heat and let it stand for 5 minutes. You should have ended up with a beautifully light and fluffy pilav. Serve the kofte accompanied with the pilav, chilli sauce, tahini yoghurt and a few leaves of crispy baby gem lettuce.
Per serving 544 cals, 14.6g fat (4.6g sat fats), 50.4g protein, 54g carbs, 19.3g sugars

··

MARINATED CHICKEN WITH TABBOULEH & LEMON YOGHURT

(Pictured on p 57)

Serves 8

- 1 tbsp chilli oil
- 2 tbsp baharat (see note)
- Zest of 1 lemon
- 1½ tsp Iranian dried lime powder (see note)
- 1 tbsp honey

- 1kg skinless and boneless chicken thigh fillets
- Pickled guindilla peppers, to serve (optional)

Tabbouleh

- 120g bulgur wheat
- 3 tomatoes, deseeded and finely chopped
- ¼ cucumber, deseeded and finely diced
- 1 large bunch of parsley, leaves picked and roughly chopped
- 1 small bunch of mint, leaves picked and roughly chopped
- 1 tsp allspice
- 1 pomegranate, seeds only
- Zest and juice of 1 lemon
- 2 tbsp extra-virgin olive oil
- 1 tsp chilli flakes

Lemon yoghurt

- 1 tbsp tahini
- Juice of 2 lemons
- 200g greek yoghurt
- 1 garlic clove, peeled and crushed
- Extra-virgin olive oil, to serve

1 Mix the chilli oil, baharat, lemon zest, dried lime and honey in a bowl. Season, stir in the chicken and leave in the fridge to marinate for at least 1 hour, or ideally overnight.
2 Preheat your grill to medium-hot, then grill the chicken for 12-15 minutes, turning frequently.
3 For the tabbouleh, put the bulgur wheat in a pan with 600ml of cold water. Bring to the boil, then simmer for 15 minutes, until all the water has been absorbed. Drain and leave to cool, then season and toss with the rest of the ingredients.
4 Combine all the yoghurt ingredients in a bowl. Loosen with a little water, if needed, then drizzle with oil. Serve the chicken on top of the tabbouleh with the guindilla peppers, if using.
Note Baharat is a Middle Eastern spice blend. You can buy it at ottolenghi.co.uk. Dried lime powder is stocked at greenfieldsuk.co.uk.
Per serving 321 cals, 13.6g fat (3.4g sat fats), 27.8g protein, 8.7g carbs, 4.9g sugars

new

Jamie Oliver
KEEP IT SIMPLE

NO-FUSS FOOD
full of
FLAVOUR

Ready-to-eat pulses and grains, great on their own or as part of a meal

SEE INSTORE FOR THE FULL RANGE

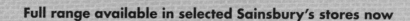

Full range available in selected Sainsbury's stores now

MEAT

Fiddes Payne

HOT & SOUR BEEF NOODLE SALAD

HOT & SOUR BEEF NOODLE SALAD

Serves 4 (DF) (GF)

- Juice of 2 limes, plus wedges to serve
- 1 tbsp thai red curry paste
- 2 sirloin steaks
- 4 tbsp sweet chilli sauce
- 1 tsp fish sauce
- 2-3 bird's-eye chillies, finely sliced
- 300g ready-cooked rice noodles
- 4 carrots, peeled
- 2 cucumbers, deseeded
- A handful each of chopped coriander and mint leaves

1 Mix 1 tablespoon of the lime juice with the red curry paste and rub all over the steaks. Heat a non-stick griddle or frying pan over a high heat and sear the steaks for 2 minutes on each side, for medium-rare.
2 Remove from the heat, cover and set aside to rest. Combine the rest of the lime juice with the sweet chilli sauce, fish sauce and the chilli.
3 Heat the noodles according to the packet, then place in a serving dish.
4 Slice the carrot and cucumber into thin strips and add to the noodles along with the chopped herbs. Spoon over the lime and chilli dressing. Slice the steaks into strips, reserving any juices, then add both to the noodles. Toss well and serve with lime wedges.

Per serving 503 cals, 5.9g fat (2g sat fats), 28.7g protein, 81.4g carbs, 18.9g sugars

POACHED BEEF WITH HERB VINAIGRETTE & LEEKS

POACHED BEEF WITH HERB VINAIGRETTE & LEEKS

Serves 8-10 (DF)

- 2 tbsp olive oil
- 6 onions, peeled and roughly sliced
- 200ml white wine
- 3 litres vegetable stock
- 6 leeks, halved lengthways
- 1.25kg beef-eye fillet, roughly 8cm in diameter

Herb vinaigrette

- 1 tsp dijon mustard
- 2 tsp wine vinegar
- 1 tsp savora sauce (see note)
- 4 tbsp rapeseed oil
- 1 shallot, finely chopped
- 6 cornichons, finely chopped
- 1 tsp capers
- A bunch each of coriander and chives, finely chopped

1 Heat the olive oil in a flameproof casserole pan over a high heat and cook the onions for 15 minutes, until browned. Deglaze with the wine, then pour in the vegetable stock. Add leeks and cook for 30 minutes.
2 Tie the beef with kitchen string at 2cm intervals, then attach to each end of a wooden spoon to make a handle – the string should be long enough so that the spoon can be balanced on top of the pan while the beef is submerged in the stock.
3 Lower the beef into the pan and poach over a low-medium heat for 15 minutes for rare (20 for medium, 25 for well done). Take the pan off the heat and transfer the beef to a warm plate. Cover with foil and allow to rest for 5-10 minutes. Drain the leeks and keep them warm.
4 In a bowl, combine the dijon mustard, vinegar, savora sauce and rapeseed oil, then add the shallot, cornichons, capers, coriander and chives, and season to taste.
5 Slice the beef very thinly, drizzle over the herb vinaigrette and serve with the leeks on the side.

Note Savora, or sauce saveur Amora, is a French mustard sauce, slightly sweetened with honey. Find it at French supermarkets or online at amazon.co.uk. Alternatively, add 1 tsp of honey to the dijon mustard.

Per serving 438 cals, 23.7g fat (6.9g sat fats), 38.6g protein, 13.8g carbs, 10g sugars

MIDDLE EASTERN LAMB

- 90g pork mince
- 90g chicken livers, chopped
- 1 onion, peeled and finely chopped
- 3-4 sage leaves, finely chopped
- 2 sprigs of thyme, leaves picked
- 2 sprigs of rosemary, leaves picked and chopped
- 10g pine nuts
- 15g sultanas
- 100g mortadella, sliced
- 2-3 tbsp olive oil
- 2 carrots
- 1 small onion
- 175ml white wine
- 35ml vin santo

Garlic & rosemary potatoes

- 50ml olive oil
- 500g potatoes, peeled and cutinto large chunks
- 3 sprigs of rosemary, leaves picked
- 3 garlic cloves, skin on, smashed

1 Preheat the oven to 220C/gas 7. Season the pork loin, add the lemon zest and rub into the meat. Set aside. 2 Place the bread in a bowl, cover with 100ml of water and leave to soak for 10 minutes. Drain, squeeze out the excess water, then mix in the parmesan, pork mince, livers, onion, herbs, pine nuts and sultanas, and season. Spread the mixture all over the loin, cover with the mortadella, then roll up and tie with string. Rub all over with olive oil and season. 3 Place the carrots, onion, wine, vin santo and 60ml of water in a roasting tin, then sit the pork on top. Roast for 30 minutes, then turn the oven down to 150C/gas 2 and cook for 3 hours. 4 Place the potatoes in a medium-sized pan, cover with cold water and bring to the boil over a medium heat. Cook for 10-15 minutes, until just tender, then drain and set aside. 5 About 30 minutes before the meat is done, heat the oil in a large frying pan. Add the potatoes and cook for 5-7 minutes. Stir in the rosemary and garlic then sauté until the potatoes are cooked, golden and crispy. 6 Once the meat is cooked, let it rest for 5 minutes, then serve with the rosemary and garlic potatoes.

Per serving 777 cals, 51.9g fat (16.6g sat fats), 46.7g protein, 28.3g carbs, 6.1g sugars

MIDDLE-EASTERN LAMB

Serves 4

- 600g lamb neck fillet
- 2 tbsp harissa
- 1 tsp za'atar
- 2 tbsp pomegranate molasses
- 2 red onions, quartered
- 6 garlic cloves, bashed
- ½ bunch of parsley, leaves picked, stalks finely chopped
- Flatbreads, salad and greek yoghurt, to serve

1 Preheat the oven to 200C/gas 6. Rub the lamb with harissa, za'atar and molasses. Season. 2 Place the onions, garlic and parsley stalks in a snug roasting tin and top with the lamb. Cook for 15 minutes, then pour over 100ml of boiling water. Cover tightly with foil, reduce the heat to 160C/gas 2-3 and cook for 1 hour, until the meat is tender. Let it rest for 10 minutes. 3 Pull the meat apart with two forks, sprinkle with the parsley leaves and pan juices and serve with the breads, salad and yoghurt.

Per serving 381 cals, 22.6g fat (9.8g sat fats), 31.2g protein, 13.2g carbs, 9.6g sugars

PORCHETTA WITH GARLIC & ROSEMARY POTATOES

An epic roast. Porchetta is technically pork loin and belly, though this recipe just uses loin.

Serves 8

- 1.5kg pork loin, deboned and butterflied (ask your butcher to do this for you)
- Zest of 1 lemon
- 175g bread
- 10g parmesan, grated

KOFTA-STYLE LAMB MEATBALLS
WITH DILL YOGURT

KOFTA-STYLE LAMB MEATBALLS WITH DILL YOGHURT

Makes approx 24

- 1 tbsp cumin seeds
- 1 tbsp coriander seeds
- 500g lamb mince
- 1 tbsp dried mint
- 1 tsp sumac
- 2 garlic cloves, peeled and crushed
- 1 tbsp harissa
- 50g fresh breadcrumbs
- 50g dried apricots, roughly chopped
- 1 medium egg, beaten

Dill yoghurt
- 250g greek yoghurt
- 2 tbsp chopped pistachios
- 3 tbsp chopped dill
- ½ tsp sumac
- Warm flatbreads to serve

1 Preheat the grill to medium-hot. Toast the cumin and coriander seeds in a small pan for a few minutes. Tip into a pestle and mortar and crush.
2 For the kofta, place the crushed spices, mince, mint, sumac, garlic, harissa, breadcrumbs, apricots and egg in a bowl, along with a good pinch of pepper and sea salt, and mix well with your hands. Form into 24 walnut-sized balls, then put in the fridge to chill for 30 minutes.
3 Take eight metal skewers, thread three balls onto each one and flatten so the kebab has two obvious sides. Grill for 4-5 minutes on each side.
4 Meanwhile, mix the yoghurt with the pistachios and dill, then scrape into a small bowl and scatter with sumac and a pinch of salt and pepper.
5 Take the koftas off the skewers and serve with the yoghurt and warm flatbreads, if you like, plus cocktail sticks to skewer the meat.
Per serving 77 cals, 5.2g fat (1.9g sat fats), 5.8g protein, 2.5g carbs, 1.3g sugars

PORK RIBS WITH SWEET & SOUR GOOSEBERRIES

PORK RIBS WITH SWEET & SOUR GOOSEBERRIES

Serves 4-6

- 2 tbsp chinese five spice, plus an extra pinch
- 4 tbsp soft light brown sugar
- 2 tbsp dark soy sauce
- 2 tbsp hoisin sauce
- 1 rack of pork belly ribs (1.75kg), separated
- 350g gooseberries
- 50ml orange juice
- 1 tbsp rice wine vinegar

Pickled salad
- 2 spring onions, cut into sticks
- 50g beanshoots
- 1 carrot, cut into thin sticks
- Juice of ½ lime, wedges to serve
- 1 tbsp rice wine vinegar
- A pinch of soft light brown sugar
- A small handful of coriander, chopped
- A small handful of mint, leaves picked

1 Preheat the oven to 180C/gas 4. Combine the chinese five spice, 2 tablespoons of the brown sugar, the soy and hoisin sauce in a large bowl, then rub all over the pork ribs, holding back a little of the marinade to use later. Season well.
2 Wrap the ribs in a double layer of foil, then roast in a roasting tin for about 1 hour, until the meat is tender. Remove from the foil and place in the tin. Brush the pork with the remaining marinade and cook for another 30-40 minutes, until sticky.
3 Place the gooseberries in a pan with the orange juice, wine vinegar and remaining sugar. Simmer for 10 minutes, until the gooseberries begin to pop, then add the extra five spice. Mix all the salad ingredients in a bowl, then serve with the pork ribs, gooseberries and lime wedges.
Per serving 951 cals, 59.5g fat (22.8g sat fats), 84.1g protein, 23.2g carbs, 22.3g sugars

RAS EL HANOUT LAMB
SKEWERS & TABBOULEH

little olive oil. Cut the last lemon half
into wedges and serve with the lamb,
bulgur, tomatoes and yoghurt.

Per serving 522 cals, 26.6g fat (8.2g sat
fats), 23.2g protein, 14.7g carbs, 5.9g sugars

....

PHO WITH BEEF
Serves 6 ⒹⒻ

- 1 tbsp sunflower oil
- 4 garlic cloves, peeled and sliced
- 1 thumb-sized piece of ginger,
  peeled and roughly sliced
- 2 lemongrass stalks, bashed
- 4 star anise
- 2.4 litres fresh beef stock
- 2 tbsp fish sauce, or to taste
- 1 tbsp palm sugar
- 500g beef bavette or sirloin
- 500g rice noodles

Salad

- A large bunch of coriander,
  leaves picked
- 400g beansprouts
- Juice of 1 large lime, plus extra
  wedges to serve
- 2 green chillies, sliced
- 2 red chillies, sliced
- A large bunch of thai basil,
  leaves picked
- 80g peanuts, roasted
  and crushed

RAS EL HANOUT LAMB
SKEWERS & TABBOULEH
**Sun shining? You could also cook
these skewers on the barbecue.**
Serves 4

- 400g lamb leg, trimmed and
  diced into 2.5cm chunks
- 2 tsp ras el hanout
- Extra-virgin olive oil, plus extra
  for drizzling
- 150g bulgur wheat
- 300g cherry tomatoes,
  on the vine
- ½ small bunch each of coriander
  and mint
- Seeds of 1 pomegranate
- 1 lemon, halved
- 150g plain yoghurt

1 Preheat the oven to 190C/gas 5.
Toss the diced lamb in a bowl with
the ras el hanout and 1 tablespoon

of olive oil. Cover and leave in the
fridge to marinate.
2 Meanwhile, rinse the bulgur wheat
and cook according to the packet.
3 Place the cherry tomatoes on a
baking tray with a drizzle of olive oil
and a pinch of salt and pepper. Roast
in the oven for 15 minutes, until
soft, then set aside.
4 Once the bulgur is cooked, drain
and rinse under cold water. Place in
a large serving bowl.
5 Preheat a griddle pan over a high
heat. Thread the lamb onto skewers.
Griddle for 8-10 minutes, turning
occasionally, until lightly charred.
6 Chop the herbs, reserving some
to garnish, and toss with the bulgur,
pomegranate seeds, 2 tablespoons
of oil, the juice from half the lemon
and a pinch of salt and pepper.
Season the yoghurt and swirl in a

1 Heat the oil in a large pan over
a medium heat, then fry the garlic,
ginger, lemongrass and star anise
for 2 minutes, until soft. Stir in the
stock, fish sauce and sugar. Bring to
the boil, then simmer for 15 minutes,
until fragrant. Check carefully for
seasoning, adding a little extra fish
sauce if necessary.
2 Meanwhile, put a griddle pan over
a high heat. Season your beef and
sear for 2 minutes on each side (for
medium rare). Rest on a board for
1 minute, then slice at an angle.
3 Prepare the rice noodles according
to the packet. Meanwhile, combine
all of the salad ingredients in a bowl.
4 Divide the noodles between six
serving bowls, ladle over the stock
and top with the beef. Serve with
peanut salad and lime wedges.
Per serving 693 cals, 20.5g fat (6.2g sat
fats), 46.2g protein, 78.4g carbs, 6.7g sugars

PHO WITH BEEF

PORK & BLACK BEANS

Serves 4 (DF)

- 2 tbsp shaoxing rice wine
- 1 tbsp sesame oil
- 2 tsp cornflour
- 3 tbsp reduced-salt soy sauce
- 400g pork fillet, sliced into discs about 1cm thick
- ½ bunch of spring onions, white parts sliced on the diagonal, green parts sliced into ribbons
- 2 green peppers, deseeded and each half cut into 8
- 2 tbsp groundnut oil
- 1 tbsp chilli oil
- 5 garlic cloves, peeled and very thinly sliced
- 1 long red chilli, sliced on the diagonal
- 1 tsp dried chilli flakes (optional)
- A thumb-sized piece of ginger, peeled, chopped into matchsticks
- 1 tsp soft brown sugar
- 2 tbsp asian fermented black beans (see note)
- Cooked jasmine rice and 1 tbsp sesame seeds, toasted, to serve

1 Combine the wine, oil, cornflour and 1 tablespoon of soy sauce. Add the pork and leave to marinate.
2 In a bowl, cover the spring onions with ice-cold water and set aside.
3 Heat a large wok until smoking hot. Add the peppers and fry for 4 minutes, or until slightly charred.
4 Add 1 tablespoon of groundnut oil to the wok and stir to coat the peppers. Leave for 1 minute, then transfer the peppers onto a plate.
5 Lift the pork out of the marinade and carefully add to the wok. Stir-fry for 3–4 minutes, moving it every 20 seconds or so. Transfer the meat to a plate and set aside.
6 Add the rest of the groundnut oil and the chilli oil to the wok. Add the garlic, chilli, dried chilli, ginger and white part of the spring onion, then stir-fry for 30 seconds.
7 Stir in the sugar, 3 tablespoons of water and remaining soy sauce. Bring to the boil and return the pork and peppers to the wok. Add the black beans, then stir-fry for 3 minutes.
8 Serve with the jasmine rice and

PORK BURGERS WITH RHUBARB KETCHUP

garnish with the sesame seeds and the green part of the spring onion.
Note Fermented black beans are soy beans that have been preserved in salt. Find them in asian supermarkets or at theasiancookshop.co.uk.
Per serving 305 cals, 18.7g fat (3.9g sat fats), 25.8g protein, 8.5g carbs, 5.2g sugars

PORK BURGERS WITH RHUBARB KETCHUP

Serves 4 (DF)

- 500g pork mince
- 1 onion, peeled and finely chopped
- 8 sprigs of thyme, leaves only
- 4 burger baps, split
- Little gem lettuce leaves and red onion rings, to serve

Rhubarb ketchup

- 700g rhubarb
- 1 onion, peeled and chopped
- 125ml cider vinegar
- 75g light muscovado sugar
- 400g tin chopped tomatoes
- 1 cinnamon stick
- 2 tsp pickling spice, in a tea infuser

1 Put the ketchup ingredients in a non-aluminium pan. Add ½ teaspoon of salt and bring to a gentle simmer over a low heat. Cook for 1 hour, then remove the spices and blitz the ketchup in a blender. Allow to cool.
2 Mix the pork, onion and thyme in a bowl, season, then shape into four patties. Chill for 10 minutes. Preheat a griddle over a medium heat.
3 Cook the patties for 5 minutes on each side. Lightly toast the baps, then fill with lettuce, onion, patties and a dollop of the rhubarb ketchup.
Per serving 421 cals, 16g fat (4.8g sat fats), 31.4g protein, 38.4g carbs, 11.8g sugars

Most of us love a nice bit of meat, but the trend these days is to cut back on how much we eat, and instead opt for better quality. So you want to ensure there are loads of other great flavours happening on your plate as well. Jamie Oliver's range of ready-to-cook grains and pulses keep things quick and simple but add incredible taste and textures. Try curried chickpeas alongside a lamb tagine, sweet chilli spelt with barbecued beef kebabs, or serve steak with tomato and olive quinoa. Keep packs at work to pop in the microwave, ready to bulk up a salad or any meaty leftovers

BRAISED SHORT RIB WITH YUKON GOLD MASH
Serves 4 (GF)
- 220g sugar
- 220g salt
- 2kg short rib of beef
- Vegetable oil
- 3 large onions, peeled, 2 sliced into rings, 1 finely chopped
- Olive oil
- 1 celery stalk, finely chopped
- 1 carrot, finely chopped
- A few sprigs of thyme
- 1 bay leaf
- 350ml red wine
- Wild garlic leaves, crispy shallots and grated cheddar, to serve

Calçots
- 8 calçots or 12 spring onions (see note)
- 125ml lemon juice (about 4 lemons)
- 200ml olive oil
- 60g sugar
- 60g salt

Mash
- 1kg potatoes, preferably yukon gold, peeled and evenly chopped
- 50g butter
- A splash of milk (optional)

1 To make your brine, combine the sugar, salt and 3.5 litres of water in a very large non-metallic pan. Add the short rib of beef and leave to soak for 10-12 hours.
2 Preheat the oven to 150C/gas 2. Heat a splash of vegetable oil in a large saucepan. Add the onion rings with a splash of water and pop the lid on. Cook over a gentle, low heat for 20-25 minutes, until the onions are soft, stirring occasionally. Be careful not to let them colour or burn.

3 Drain the short rib and pat dry with kitchen towel. Heat a little veg oil in a frying pan over a medium-high heat, then fry the meat, making sure to get proper colour on it without burning. Remove from the pan and set aside.
4 Add a drizzle of olive oil to the same pan, then fry the finely chopped onion, celery, carrot, thyme and bay leaf over a medium heat until tender and golden. Pour in the red wine to deglaze the pan.
5 Tip the onion confit, 100ml water and the short rib into an oven dish that snugly fits the meat. Cover with tinfoil and roast for 4-5 hours, until the meat is falling off the bone and the fat has broken down. Check it after 3½ hours: if the meat is almost ready, it should begin to break apart easily when you put pressure on it; if it is still springy and doesn't start to fall apart, it will need another hour or so in the oven.
6 Soak the calçots in water for 10 minutes (skip this if using spring onions), then drain, trim the ends and rub all over to remove any grit. In a pan, combine 500ml of water with the lemon juice, olive oil, sugar and salt. Add the calçots or spring onions and simmer with the lid on for 7-8 minutes, until tender.
7 For the mash, simmer the potatoes in a pan of salted water until cooked, about 15 minutes. Mash them well or press through a ricer, then mix in the butter. Loosen with milk, if needed. Season to taste.
8 Remove the ribs from the pan, then discard the bones and any large pieces of fat. Cut into four.
9 Spoon the mash onto serving plates, top with the rich beef and

serve with the calçots on the side. Scatter over the wild garlic leaves, crispy shallots and grated cheddar.
Note Calçots are large Catalan spring onions. Find them at natoora.co.uk.
Per serving 1,087 cals, 64.1g fat (28.9g sat fats), 54.3g protein, 62.5g carbs, 17g sugars

....

MINCED LAMB, CHICKPEA & SPINACH RICE
(not pictured)
Serves 4
- 2 tbsp olive oil
- 400g minced lamb
- 1 onion, peeled and chopped
- 3 garlic cloves, peeled and crushed
- ¼ tsp cinnamon
- 2 tbsp mild or medium curry powder
- 500g cooked brown basmati rice
- 400g tin chickpeas, drained
- 250ml vegetable or chicken stock
- 80g baby spinach leaves
- Plain yoghurt, to serve

1 Heat the oil in a wide, non-stick saucepan over a medium heat, then add the lamb, onion, garlic, cinnamon and curry powder and stir-fry for 10 minutes, or until the lamb is browned and the onion softened.
2 Add the rice, chickpeas and stock, bring to the boil over a high heat, then reduce the heat to medium. Season, cover and simmer for 5 minutes, or until the rice is hot.
3 Remove the pan from the heat and stir in the spinach. Cover and stand for 5-8 minutes to wilt the spinach, then serve with a dollop of yoghurt.
Per serving 621 cals, 24.6g fat (8g sat fats), 32g protein, 71.6g carbs, 4.2g sugars

BRAISED SHORT RIB
WITH YUKON GOLD MASH

LAMB, FETA & COURGETTE BURGERS

LAMB, FETA & COURGETTE BURGERS

Serves 4

- 400g lamb mince
- ½ courgette, coarsely grated
- Finely grated zest of ½ lemon
- A small handful of parsley, finely chopped
- 50g feta, crumbled
- 1 egg yolk
- 1 tbsp english mustard
- 1 tbsp tomato ketchup
- 3 tbsp yoghurt
- 3 gherkins, chopped
- 1 iceburg lettuce, chopped
- Olive oil
- 4 burger buns

1 In a large bowl, mix together the lamb, courgette, lemon zest, parsley, feta and egg yolk, then season with a generous pinch of salt and pepper. Using wet hands, form the mixture into four burgers.
2 Combine the mustard, ketchup and yoghurt, then stir through the gherkins and lettuce. Set aside.
3 Pop a large frying pan over a medium heat, rub the burgers with a little oil and place in the pan. Cook each side for 4–5 minutes, or until just cooked through.
4 Split your buns and place them cut-side down in the frying pan, to soak up the lovely cooking juices, then fill each with the lamb burgers and crunchy relish.

Per serving 454 cals, 21.4g fat (9.3g sat fats), 29.4g protein, 35.8g carbs, 6.8g sugars

STICKY PORK & NECTARINE SKEWERS

STICKY PORK & NECTARINE SKEWERS

Serves 4 DF

- Juice of 1 lemon, zest of ½
- 2 tbsp dark soy sauce
- 2 tbsp sweet chilli sauce
- 2 tbsp runny honey
- 4 nectarines, halved, destoned and cut into large chunks
- 600g lean pork tenderloin or fillet, trimmed of fat and cut into large chunks
- 4 pak choi, halved or quartered
- 1 tbsp olive oil

1 Preheat a griddle pan or barbecue to medium-high. Reserve 1 tablespoon of the lemon juice, then add the rest to a bowl with the zest, dark soy sauce, sweet chilli sauce and honey. Add the nectarines and pork and marinate for at least 10 minutes.

2 Once marinated, thread the chunks of meat and nectarine onto eight metal skewers, then set aside on a plate until you're ready to cook.
3 Pour the remaining marinade into a pan and gently simmer over a medium heat until reduced by half.
4 Place the skewers on the griddle or barbecue for 10–12 minutes, turning and brushing with the sticky, reduced marinade, until cooked.
5 Blanch the pak choi in a pan of lightly salted boiling water for 2–3 minutes, or until just wilted, then drain and place in a bowl.
6 Whisk the rest of the lemon juice with the olive oil, then drizzle this over the pak choi. Toss together well and serve with the sticky barbecued pork skewers.

Per serving 320 cals, 9.1g fat (2.3g sat fats), 35.7g protein, 24.6g carbs, 24.1g sugars

NO-FUSS FOOD

This range of ready-to-eat store-cupboard essentials from Jamie Oliver provides you with a base that you can call on to transform any dish, and a brilliant way to create a meal when you're short on time. Be it preparing fresh veggies and salads or roasting a leg of lamb to perfection, whipping up a healthy, full-of-flavour feast has never been easier.

INCREDIBLE CURRIED CHICKPEAS

These are gorgeous served as a side dish with your favourite curry or spicy chilli. Stir through cooked spinach and yoghurt to cool things down a little! Alternatively, mix into a tasty kale salad with toasted seeds, feta cheese and roasted root veg.

Jamie Oliver

ALOHA BOYO KEBABS

ALOHA BOYO KEBABS

This recipe, from southern-style barbecue vendors Hangfire Smokehouse, marries the native flavours of Hawaii with beautiful Welsh lamb and leeks.

Serves 4 (DF)

- 1kg boneless leg or shoulder of Welsh lamb (800g prepared weight), trimmed and cut into 5cm cubes (ask your butcher to bone it for you)
- 1 ripe pineapple, peeled, cored and cut into 5cm cubes
- Vegetable oil
- Salad and flatbreads, to serve

Dipping sauce
- 30g coriander, chopped
- 30g flat-leaf parsley, chopped
- ½ red chili pepper, deseeded and finely chopped
- Juice of ½ lime
- 3 tbsp olive oil

Lamb marinade
- 3 garlic cloves, peeled and roughly chopped
- ¼ small leek, roughly chopped
- 1 red chilli pepper, roughly chopped
- ½ thumb-sized piece of fresh ginger, peeled and chopped
- 250ml fresh pineapple juice

- 50ml dark soy sauce
- 3 tbsp sesame oil
- Juice of ½ lime
- 1 tbsp soft light brown sugar

1 Place all the marinade ingredients, except the sugar, in a food processor and blend until smooth. Put the marinade and lamb into a large, sealable plastic bag. Massage the marinade into the meat through the bag, ensuring it is well covered. Leave in the fridge for 3-5 hours, or overnight for more flavour.
2 Once the meat has marinated, drain the liquid into a pan, bring it to the boil, then simmer for about 10 minutes or until reduced by half. Add the soft light brown sugar and stir until dissolved and glossy.
3 Take some bamboo or metal skewers - if you use bamboo, soak them in water for a couple of hours to stop them burning as you grill. Thread the cubes of lamb and pineapple onto the skewers, alternating meat and fruit.
4 Preheat the grill, whether you're using charcoal or gas. It must be hot, so turn the gas up high or make sure the coals are white hot. Brush a little vegetable oil on the grilling grates to stop the kebabs from sticking.
5 Depending on how you like to eat your lamb, grill the skewers for 2-3 minutes on each side, brushing with the marinade each time you turn them. This will give you medium-rare lamb. If you like yours a little more well done, add another minute's cooking time to each side.
6 To cook indoors, preheat a grill pan to medium-high. Grill the skewers for 2-3 minutes on each side for a total of 8-10 minutes, brushing with the reduced marinade each time you turn.
7 Make the dipping sauce by combining the coriander, parsley, chilli pepper, lime juice and olive oil in a bowl. Set the skewers on a plate, drizzle the herby mixture on top, or leave on the side. Serve with warm flatbreads and a seasonal salad.
Per serving 871 cals, 65.8g fat (24.1g sat fats), 46.1g protein, 25.5g carbs, 24.8g sugars

ANDALUSIAN-STYLE GRILLED LAMB CUTLETS
(pictured on p57)

Lamb is a favourite in Spanish cooking. These grilled spiced cutlets are moreish, and perfect served with zingy chickpea salad.
Serves 4 (DF) (GF)
- 8 lamb cutlets
- Rock salt

Marinade
- 2 tsp sweet smoked paprika
- 2 tsp ground cumin
- 1 tsp dried oregano
- 1 tsp turmeric powder
- 10 sprigs of thyme
- 2 garlic cloves, peeled and finely chopped
- A generous drizzle of olive oil

Chickpea salad
- 400g tin of chickpeas, drained and rinsed
- 1 small bunch of flat-leaf parsley, roughly chopped
- ½ red onion, peeled and thinly sliced
- A handful of green olives, destoned and roughly chopped
- 1 tbsp sherry vinegar
- A generous drizzle of olive oil
- 1 tbsp honey
- ½ tsp cumin powder
- 1 fresh red chilli, deseeded and finely chopped

1 Start by preparing your marinade. Mix all the ingredients together (you don't need to chop the thyme) in a non-reactive bowl. Add the cutlets and rub in the marinade using your hands. Pop in the fridge for at least a couple of hours, or overnight.
2 Then, just before you cook your lamb, make the chickpea salad. Toss all the ingredients together in a large bowl, then set aside until ready to serve. Preheat the grill to high.
3 Season both sides of the cutlets with rock salt and grill them for 1½ minutes each side, then repeat (6 minutes in total). Allow the cutlets to rest for 1-2 minutes before serving with the chickpea salad.
Per serving 394 cals, 26g fat (10g sat fats), 18.8g protein, 22.9g carbs, 5.8g sugars

PACKED FULL OF FLAVOUR

Wholesome grains and pulses are a nutritious addition to any dish, but can be a hassle to cook. Jamie Oliver's delicious blends save time, so you can concentrate on preparing a tip-top meal that tastes great and saves you time.

SUPER TOMATO & OLIVE QUINOA

Try this hot with a little squeeze of lemon juice and some chopped fresh parsley and mint – it's delicious with grilled meat or prawns. Quinoa has the highest protein content of all wholegrains, so it's also perfect for a veggie option. Try with marinated and grilled peppers, courgettes and aubergines and some crumbled goat's cheese for a simple, delicious midweek supper.

DESSERTS

Yeo Valley
FAMILY FARM

QUESADA PASIEGA
(Cantabrian cheesecake)

'Pasiega' refers to an area of Cantabria, northern Spain, known for its dairy produce. This light, crustless cheesecake is crazily good served with roasted apricots.

Serves 8-10 ⓥ

- 100g unsalted butter, softened, plus extra for greasing
- 325g golden caster sugar
- 3 large eggs
- 1 vanilla pod, seeds only
- 300g ricotta cheese
- 500ml whole milk
- 180g plain flour
- Finely grated zest of 1 lemon
- 400g fresh apricots, halved and destoned
- 125ml sweet sherry
- 4 tbsp runny honey
- A couple of rosemary sprigs, leaves picked, plus another ½ sprig to garnish

1 Preheat the oven to 180C/gas 4. Grease a round 20cm cake tin and line the base with baking paper.
2 Using a free-standing mixer or an electric hand whisk, cream the butter for 2 minutes, until pale. Add the sugar and whisk until smooth and light. Beat in the eggs, one by one, then stir in the vanilla seeds, ricotta and a pinch of salt. Stir in the milk.
3 Fold in the flour and zest. Pour into the greased tin and bake for 50-55 minutes, until golden and set but still a bit wobbly in the centre. Cool in the tin for at least 30 minutes.
4 Turn the oven up to 220C/gas 7. Lay the apricots in a snug ovenproof dish, cut-side up. Drizzle over the sherry and honey, then scatter over the rosemary. Roast for 20 minutes, basting a couple of times.
5 Top the quesada with the apricots and garnish with the rosemary.

Per serving 513 cals, 18g fat (10g sat fats), 11g protein, 77g carbs, 60g sugars

EARL GREY-INFUSED ICE CREAM

EARL GREY-INFUSED ICE CREAM

Serves 6 ⓥ

- 250ml whole milk
- 125g sugar
- 500ml double cream
- 2 tbsp loose earl grey tea leaves
- 5 egg yolks
- 4 shortbread biscuits, crumbled

1 Put the milk, sugar and cream in a large pan over a low-medium heat, then stir continuously until the sugar has dissolved and the liquid is steaming, about 10 minutes. Stir in the tea leaves, then remove from the heat and cover. Leave the tea to infuse for 10 minutes. Carefully pour the mixture through a sieve into a bowl, squeezing the loose tea really well to extract all the flavour. Discard the leaves and set the liquid aside.

2 In a large bowl, whisk the egg yolks until they are light and fluffy. Slowly add the milk mixture, whisking continuously (so it doesn't split) until the mixture is combined. Return to the pan and stir over a medium heat for around 5 minutes, until the mixture has thickened and coats the back of the spoon, like custard.
3 Place in an ice-cream machine and churn according to the manufacturer's instructions, until chilled and starting to solidify. Transfer the ice cream to a container then put in the freezer until it's completely frozen. Remove from the freezer 5 minutes before serving to allow it to soften slightly, then serve topped with the crumbled shortbread biscuits.

Per serving 547 cals, 41.8g fat (26g sat fats), 7.6g protein, 37.3g carbs, 29.4g sugars

RASPBERRY & GINGER CHEESECAKE

RASPBERRY & GINGER CHEESECAKE
Serves 12 (v)

- 350g gingernut biscuits
- 150g unsalted butter, melted
- 2 large eggs, separated
- 2 tbsp golden caster sugar
- 500g mascarpone
- 1 tsp vanilla extract
- 250g raspberries

1 Line a 32 x 22cm dish (about 4cm deep) with cling film, leaving some overhang. Blitz the biscuits into fine crumbs in a food processor, then stir in the butter. Pour into the tin and push into the sides and bottom. Set in the fridge for at least 1 hour.
2 In a bowl, whisk the egg yolks and sugar until creamy, then fold in the mascarpone and vanilla. In a separate bowl, beat the egg whites into stiff peaks, then fold into the mascarpone mixture. Mash 150g of the raspberries in a bowl, then stir them in, too, creating a rippled effect with a spoon or fork.
3 Pour into the lined tin and chill in the fridge for 2 hours. Use the cling film to carefully lift the cheesecake out of the dish, then serve with the rest of the raspberries on top.
Per serving 421 cals, 32.8g fat (20.9g sat fats), 4.7g protein, 28.8g carbs, 16g sugars

....

MALT CUSTARD & LOGANBERRY TART
Utterly addictive, the malt adds a really nostalgic edge. The trick is to cook the pastry to a deep golden brown. You'll need to use a cook's blowtorch to caramelise the top of the tart.

Serves 10 (v)
- 10 large egg yolks
- 75g golden caster sugar
- 750ml double cream
- 175g malt extract
- 60g loganberry (or you can use raspberry) jam
- Demerara sugar, to finish

Pastry
- 250g flour
- 50g icing sugar
- 125g cold unsalted butter, cubed
- 2 large eggs, 1 beaten
- 30ml milk

1 Make a malt custard: whisk the yolks and sugar until smooth and shiny. In a pan, bring the cream and malt to the boil. Off the heat, slowly pour over the egg mixture, whisking to combine. Push the mixture through a fine sieve, cover the surface with cling film, and reserve.
2 To make the pastry, rub the flour, sugar and butter into coarse crumbs. Beat the whole egg and the milk together, then mix into the crumbs to form a rough dough. Be careful not to overmix, or you'll spoil the texture. Chill the dough overnight or for at least 2 hours in the fridge.
3 Roll out to 2mm and line a 23cm, deep tart case, pressing down into the sides. Leave an overhang of dough and prick the base with a fork. Top with baking paper and fill with baking beans, then freeze for 1 hour.
4 Bake the tart at 160C/gas 2–3 for 20 minutes. Remove the beans and paper, then bake for 15-20 minutes, until golden. Brush with beaten egg and bake for 3 minutes, then leave to cool completely. Trim the pastry with a small serrated knife. Lower the oven to 120C/gas ¼–½.
5 Spread the pastry base with the jam. Fill with custard and bake on a baking tray for 4 hours, until set but with a slight wobble. Allow to cool, then chill for at least 2 hours. To serve, sprinkle the demerara sugar on the tart, then caramelise with a cook's blowtorch until golden.
Per serving 650 cals, 47g fat (28g sat fats), 11g protein, 48.6g carbs, 23.6g sugars

MALT CUSTARD &
LOGANBERRY TART

APPLE & APRICOT POTS

MANGO, CARDAMOM & YOGHURT FOOL

MAPLE GRILLED PEACHES WITH FROZEN YOGHURT

Celebrating summer stone fruit, this dessert is on the right side of indulgent.
Serves 4 ⓥ

- 6 ripe peaches, halved and stoned
- 1 tbsp melted butter
- 75ml maple syrup
- 1 tsp finely ground cardamom seeds
- 4 scoops of frozen vanilla yoghurt

1 Brush the cut sides of the peaches with the melted butter, then place, cut-side down, onto a hot griddle pan or frying pan for 3–4 minutes. Turn them over, brush with maple syrup and sprinkle with the cardamom.
2 Cook for another 3–4 minutes, until golden, sticky and tender. Place three peach halves in each serving bowl, alongside a scoop of frozen yoghurt and a good drizzle of the remaining maple syrup.
Per serving 215 cals, 8.2g fat (4.9g sat fats), 3.4g protein, 33.9g carbs, 32.1g sugars

APPLE & APRICOT POTS

Serves 4 ⒢ ⓥ

- 300g ready-to-eat dried apricots, roughly chopped
- 1 apple, skinned, cored and cut into 1cm cubes
- 175ml clear apple juice
- ½ tsp cinnamon
- ¼ tsp mixed spice
- 220g fat-free fromage frais
- 2 tbsp blanched almonds, toasted and roughly chopped
- 2 tbsp runny honey

1 Place the apricots and apple in a small saucepan with the apple juice and spices. Bring to the boil and simmer gently for 15–20 minutes, until most of the liquid has been absorbed, the apricots have plumped up and the apple has softened.
2 Remove from the heat and spoon into glasses or ramekins. Spoon over the fromage frais, top with the chopped almonds, drizzle over the honey and serve straight away.
Per serving 246 cals, 2.4g fat (0.2g sat fats), 8.2g protein, 51.4g carbs, 50g sugars

MANGO, CARDAMOM & YOGHURT FOOL

Serves 4–6 ⒢ ⓥ

- 200ml double cream
- 2 tbsp sugar
- 300g plain yoghurt, whisked to loosen
- ½ tsp crushed cardamom seeds
- 400g mango, puréed

1 Combine the cream and sugar in a bowl and whisk until the mixture has thickened slightly.
2 Fold in the yoghurt with a metal spoon. In a jug, mix the cardamom seeds with the mango pulp.
3 Use a spoon or a fork to carefully stir three-quarters of the spiced mango mixture into the yoghurt, creating an attractive marbled effect. Divide the fool evenly between your serving bowls.
4 Chill in the fridge for 1–2 hours. When you are ready to serve, pour the remaining mango mixture over the dishes and serve immediately.
Per serving 396 cals, 30.2g fat (18.8g sat fats), 5g protein, 27.7g carbs, 27.4g sugars

HONEYCOMB & RASPBERRY 'VIENNETTA'

Viennetta was once the ultimate ready-to-serve dessert, but this version is something else. Start it a day or two before serving.

Serves 8-10 GF

- 200g punnet of raspberries
- 7 large eggs, separated
- 260g golden caster sugar
- 4 x 1.5g leaves of gelatin
- 375g mascarpone
- 150g 70% dark chocolate, roughly chopped, plus shavings to serve
- 30g butter

Honeycomb

- 160g golden caster sugar
- 25g honey
- 60g liquid glucose
- 1 tsp bicarbonate of soda

1 Pop your raspberries in the freezer a day or two in advance.
2 For the honeycomb, mix all of the ingredients, apart from the bicarbonate of soda, in a deep saucepan with 30ml of water, then place over a medium heat (the pan needs to be high-sided because, when you add the bicarbonate of soda, the mix will treble in volume).
3 Insert a sugar thermometer and cook, without stirring, until it reaches 170C. Whisk in the bicarbonate of soda, then remove from the heat and carefully spoon onto an oiled sheet of baking paper. Leave to cool, then smash into chunks and set aside, reserving a handful to serve.
4 Put the egg yolks and 100g of the caster sugar in a heatproof bowl, then whisk over a pan of simmering water until light and fluffy. Remove from the heat and whisk until cool.
5 Soak the gelatine in ice-cold water. Meanwhile, put the mascarpone into a large mixing bowl and beat with a spatula until smooth, then fold through the yolk mixture.
6 Put the egg whites and remaining sugar in another heatproof bowl and place over the pan of simmering water, whisking until the sugar has dissolved, then remove from the heat. Squeeze the water out of the gelatine and add it to the sweet egg whites; keep whisking until cool and you have a light, fluffy meringue. Fold into the mascarpone mixture, then spoon into a large piping bag.
7 Line a 450g loaf tin with cling film. In another heatproof bowl, set over the pan of simmering water, melt the chocolate and butter together, then spread thinly over baking paper, in three wide strips, roughly the length and width of your loaf tin. Allow to set in the fridge until ready to use.
8 Pipe a fifth of the meringue mixture into the tin. Put 1 sheet of chocolate on top and press lightly – don't worry if it breaks a little. Top with another fifth of the mixture, then a layer of honeycomb. Repeat for the rest of the ingredients, alternating the chocolate and honeycomb, finishing with chocolate. Freeze it overnight.
9 Dip the tin into warm water, then turn the dessert out onto a serving tray. Top with chocolate shavings, the reserved honeycomb and frozen raspberries, crushed.

Per serving 522 cals, 29.8g fat (18.5g sat fats), 8.2g protein, 58.2g carbs, 54.2g sugars

CHOCOLATE MOUSSE WITH PRUNES

(Pictured on p131)

Any leftover prune mixture will keep in an airtight container in the fridge for up to a month. It's delicious with rice pudding!

Serves 12-14 V

- 350g 70% dark chocolate, broken up
- 100ml double cream
- 10 eggs, separated
- 50g golden caster sugar
- Chocolate shavings, to serve

Prunes

- 500g dried prunes
- 150ml whisky
- 100ml orange juice

1 Prepare the prunes the night before: combine all the ingredients in a bowl and leave the fruit to soak up the flavours overnight.
2 The next day, melt the chocolate in a bowl set over a pan of simmering water, ensuring the bowl doesn't touch the water. Remove the bowl from the heat and allow to cool.
3 Warm the cream in a pan, then mix into the chocolate until smooth.
4 In a separate bowl, beat the egg whites and sugar with an electric whisk until light and fluffy. Whisk the yolks into the chocolate mixture, then gently fold this through the beaten egg whites.
5 Place the prunes in the base of a deep, glass trifle dish, pressing them against the sides. Pour over the mousse and allow to set in the fridge for at least 2-3 hours. Top with chocolate shavings, and serve.

Per serving 383 cals, 21.6g fat (12g sat fats), 10.2g protein, 31.1g carbs, 29g sugars

YEO VALLEY LOVES MILK

We're all familiar with Yeo Valley milk, yoghurt and butter on our supermarket shelves, but how many of us know the real story behind the name?

Yeo Valley was founded to support British family farms, and helped to set up OMSCo (Organic Milk Suppliers Cooperative), which supplies all the milk that Yeo Valley buy in, on top of that produced by their own herd.

"OMSCo was founded in 1994 by five like-minded farmers and today we have over 250 organic family farms spread across the UK," says Miles Saunders, an OMSCo farmer from Step Farm, Faringdon.

"It's farmer-owned and run and we're proud to have supplied Yeo Valley with quality organic milk from day one. This has played a key role in maintaining sustainable prices for members, enabling them to continue dairy farming from one generation to the next."

Cows that produce organic milk have a forage-based diet, meaning they are outside grazing in the fields for most of the year.

On the Yeo Valley farms they also grow clover, which helps to keep the land healthy – and this means healthy crops for the cows, so that they can produce delicious and nutritious milk all year round.

Yeo Valley care about every little drop of milk that they use, from the farm to you!

Find out more at:
yeovalley.co.uk/milklovers

COFFEE & AMARETTO PANNACOTTA

COFFEE & AMARETTO PANNACOTTA

Two of Italy's greatest simple desserts come together for this pannacotta with an affogato twist. If you don't have pannacotta moulds, you can make and serve them in decorative glasses or teacups.

Makes 6
- 4 leaves of gelatin
- 300ml semi-skimmed milk
- 40g golden caster sugar
- 300ml double cream
- 30ml amaretto

Coffee syrup
- 300ml espresso
- 100g golden caster sugar
- 100ml amaretto (optional)

1 Place the gelatine leaves in a bowl of ice-cold water and set aside.

2 Combine the milk and sugar in a saucepan and place over a medium heat. As soon as it comes to the boil, remove from the heat. Immediately squeeze any excess water out of the gelatine, add the leaves to the hot liquid and whisk the mixture until they are dissolved.

3 Stir in the cream, then the amaretto. Pour the mixture into six pannacotta moulds or sturdy glasses or teacups and leave in the fridge overnight to set.

4 Put all the syrup ingredients in a small saucepan over a medium heat. Bring to the boil then reduce the heat and allow it to thicken for 10-12 minutes. Test the consistency by placing a small amount on a chilled plate - if ithe syrup thickens, it's ready. Set aside to cool.

5 If you are using pannacotta

INSTANT MIXED MELON SORBET

EASY CHOCOLATE CHIP COOKIES
Makes 14

- 150g Yeo Valley unsalted butter, softened
- 125g soft light brown sugar
- 100g caster sugar
- 2 tsp vanilla extract
- 1 egg plus 1 egg yolk, both at fridge-temperature
- 300g plain flour
- ½ tsp bicarbonate of soda
- 325g milk chocolate chips

1 Preheat the oven to 170C/gas 3. Line a baking sheet with baking paper and set aside.
2 Melt the butter and let it cool slightly. Combine both sugars in a bowl then beat in the butter. Add the vanilla, egg and yolk and beat until the light and creamy.
3 Slowly mix the flour and bicarb of soda until just blended, then fold in the chocolate chips.
4 Using an ice-cream scoop, form balls from the cookie dough, and drop onto the prepared baking sheet, about 8cm apart.
5 Bake in the preheated oven for 15-17 minutes, or until the edges of the cookies are slightly toasted.
6 Leave to cool on the sheet for 5 minutes before transferring to wire racks. Enjoy with a glass of organic milk!

---

moulds, dip them in hot water for 5-10 seconds to help ease out each pudding. Pull one edge of the pannacotta away from the side of the mould then invert it onto a serving plate. (If you are using glasses or cups, don't try to invert them, leave the pannacottas as they are.) Drizzle over the coffee syrup and serve.
Per serving 341 cals, 18.7g fat (12.7g sat fats), 3.8g protein, 30g carbs, 29.9g sugars

INSTANT MIXED MELON SORBET
If you can't find charentais, you can substitue for cantelope or other small, sweet melon.
Serves 4-6 (DF) (GF) (V)
- ½ charentais melon, peeled and deseeded
- ½ honeydew melon, peeled and deseeded
- 4 tbsp runny honey
- Juice of 1 orange
- 1 tbsp mint leaves, finely chopped

1 Cut both melon halves into bite-sized pieces and place on a non-stick tray lined with baking paper. Pop into the freezer for 3-4 hours, or until the melon has frozen.
2 When you are ready to serve, place the melon in a food processor along with the honey, orange juice, mint and 200ml water. Pulse the mixture a couple of times until you have a smooth consistency. Scoop the sorbet into pre-chilled glasses or bowls and serve immediately.
Per serving 133 cals, 0.3g fat (0g sat fats), 1.7g protein, 33.1g carbs, 33.1g sugars

BAKING

magimix®

the possibilities are endless

GLUTEN-FREE HOT
CROSS MUFFINS

GLUTEN-FREE HOT CROSS MUFFINS
Makes 24 (GF) (V)

- 225g butter, softened
- 200g light muscovado sugar
- 150g ground almonds
- 100g buckwheat flour (see note)
- 1 tsp ground mixed spice
- 1½ tsp gluten-free baking powder
- ¼ tsp salt
- Zest and juice 1 large orange
- 3 large eggs, at room temperature
- 175g mixed dried fruit (ideally with candied orange in it)
- 50g dried cranberries
- 1 apple (about 125g), skin on, coarsely grated
- 100g icing sugar, sifted, plus extra for dusting

1 Heat the oven to 180C/gas 4. Line two muffin trays with paper cases or squares of baking paper. In a bowl, beat the butter and sugar with an electric beater until pale and fluffy.
2 Combine the almonds, flour, mixed spice, baking powder and salt in a bowl, then sift it on top of the creamed butter and sugar. Add the orange zest, 3 tablespoons of the juice and the eggs to the bowl as well. Beat everything together until you have a thick batter, then stir in the dried fruit, cranberries and apple.
3 Dollop the mixture into the muffin cases so they're three-quarters full. Bake for 35 minutes, then turn down the heat to 160C/gas 3 and bake for a further 20-25 minutes, until the muffins are well risen and golden, and a skewer inserted into the centre comes out clean. Leave to cool in the tin for 15 minutes, then remove to a rack to cool completely.
4 Gradually mix the icing sugar with 4-5 teaspoons of the orange juice to make a thick icing. Spoon into a piping bag with a round nozzle, or into a sandwich bag, snipping off one corner. Pipe crosses onto each muffin, dust with extra icing sugar and leave to set.
Note Buckwheat, despite its name, is not related to wheat at all and is

GREEN TEA & WHITE CHOCOLATE BROWNIES

totally gluten-free. The flour has a light nuttiness. You'll find it in most supermarkets and health food shops.
Per serving 264.5 cals, 12.1g fat (5.1g sat fats), 3.2g protein, 37.9g carbs, 33.3g sugars

GREEN TEA & WHITE CHOCOLATE BROWNIES
Matcha is a green tea powder. You can find it in most organic and health food shops.
Serves 12-14 (V)

- 110g butter, cubed
- 225g white chocolate, roughly chopped
- 200g sugar
- 3 large eggs
- 80g plain flour
- 3 tbsp matcha powder
- 30g macadamia nuts, roughly chopped

1 Preheat the oven to 200C/gas 6. Line a 20 x 20cm square cake tin with baking paper. Put the butter and 200g of the chocolate in a heatproof bowl set it over a pan of simmering water. Once both the chocolate and butter have melted, take off the heat.
2 Whisk in the sugar, then beat in the eggs, one at a time. Sift the flour and macha into the white-chocolate mixture and gently fold in with a large spoon. Mix in the macadamia nuts and the remaining chocolate, sprinkling some on top.
3 Pour into the tin and bake for 5 minutes, then cover with foil and cook for another 20-25 minutes (the middle of the brownie should still be slightly soft). Leave to cool in the tin for 30 minutes, then cut into slices.
Per serving 306 cals, 17.3g fat (8.8g sat fats), 5.4g protein, 34.5g carbs, 28.9g sugars

When making your madeleines, you could speed up the process with a Magimix Pâtissier. Blend the ingredients for 30–60 seconds, scrape the mixture from the sides of the bowl, then mix for 15 seconds more, until combined. Don't over-process your mixture though, as you will beat out all the air – this is what makes your madeleines light and fluffy! For an even better rise, refrigerate your dough overnight before baking

PLUM LATTICE PIE
(Pictured on p143)

Use up luscious sweet plums for this traditional pie. You'll want the neighbours to see this beauty cooling on your windowsill…

Serves 12 Ⓥ

- 275g plain flour
- 2 tbsp icing sugar
- 130g butter, cubed
- 2 medium egg yolks
- Egg wash (1 egg yolk, beaten with a splash of milk)
- Caster sugar, for sprinkling
- Ice cream or crème fraîche, to serve (optional)

Plum filling

- 10 plums (1.3kg), halved (larger ones quartered) and destoned
- 100g caster sugar
- 1 tsp cinnamon
- ½ tsp ground ginger
- 50g butter, cubed
- 3 tbsp cornflour
- 50g toasted flaked almonds

1 Sift the flour, icing sugar and a pinch of salt into the bowl of a food processor. Add the butter and blitz until the mixture resembles fine crumbs. Tip in the yolks along with 60ml of ice-cold water and gradually pulse the mixture into a rough dough. 2 Turn the dough out onto a clean surface and gently knead it for about 30 seconds, until smooth, adding a little extra flour if needed. Divide it into two pieces, one slightly larger than the other, then roll them out into discs. Wrap both in cling film and chill in the fridge for 30 minutes.

3 Roll out the larger piece of pastry and press into a 23cm pie tin. Trim it so you have 2.5cm overhang and chill it in the fridge until required. Roll out the remaining disc and cut out eight long, even strips, about 2.5cm wide. 4 For the filling, put the plums into a large bowl and stir in all the other ingredients (depending on how sweet the fruit is, you may wish to add a little extra sugar). 5 To assemble, pile the fruit mixture into the pie base and brush the edges with egg wash. Arrange and weave the pastry strips in a lattice pattern on top of the pie. Bring the overhanging pastry from the pie base up and over the ends of the pastry strips, pressing down to seal, then crimp it all the way around with your fingers and thumb. 6 Brush the pie all over with the egg wash and sprinkle with sugar. Pop it in the fridge to chill for 30 minutes. Preheat the oven to 200C/gas 6 and place a baking tray inside to warm up. 7 Transfer the pie to the baking tray and bake in the oven for 20 minutes, checking occasionally and rotating it if it's colouring unevenly. 8 Reduce the oven to 180C/gas 4 and bake for a further 20–30 minutes, covering with a tent of tinfoil if it's browning too quickly. 9 Remove the pie from the oven, sprinkle with extra sugar and leave to set for at least 3 hours before serving. Cut into slices and serve with ice cream or crème fraîche.

Per serving 321 cals, 17g fat (8.2g sat fats), 4.8g protein, 39.8g carbs, 20.6g sugars

RASPBERRY & HONEY MADELEINES

Makes 24 Ⓥ

- 50g unsalted butter, melted and cooled, plus extra for greasing
- 75g plain flour, sifted, plus extra for dusting
- 1 large egg
- 50g golden caster sugar, plus ½ tbsp extra
- 10g honey
- 20ml milk
- ½ tsp baking powder
- Zest of 1 unwaxed lemon
- ½ tsp rose petals (see note)
- 24 raspberries

1 Preheat the oven to 200C/gas 6. Brush a mini 24-hole madeleine tin with melted butter and dust with flour, shaking out any excess. 2 Beat the egg with the sugar until pale and frothy. In another bowl, mix the honey and milk with the cooled butter, then stir into the batter. Gradually fold in the flour, baking powder and lemon zest. Cover with cling film and leave to rest in the fridge for at least 20 minutes. 3 Meanwhile, grind the remaining ½ tablespoon of sugar and the rose petals with a pestle and mortar. Spoon the batter into the tin and press a raspberry into the centre. Bake in the oven for about 6 minutes until cooked through and lightly golden. Transfer to a wire rack to cool before dusting with the rose sugar. **Note** Waitrose stocks rose petals.

Per serving 85 cals, 4.1g fat (2.2g sat fats), 1.3g protein, 11.6g carbs, 6.7g sugars

RUGELACH (LITTLE TWISTS)

RUGELACH
(Little twists)

These croissant-shaped pastries from eastern Europe are perfect with hot chocolate.

Makes 24 Ⓥ

- 225g unsalted butter, softened
- 225g cream cheese
- 75g sugar
- 1 tsp vanilla extract
- 350g plain flour, plus extra for dusting

Filling
- 100g dark chocolate, chopped
- 100g pecans, lightly toasted and finely chopped
- 2 tsp ground cinnamon
- 75g sugar
- 6 tbsp cherry, raspberry or apricot jam

Glaze
- 1 egg, beaten
- Sugar, for sprinkling

1 To make your pastry, beat the butter and cream cheese in a mixing bowl until smooth. Add the sugar and vanilla, then mix again. Sift the flour with a pinch of salt, add to the bowl and mix until smooth and combined.
2 Tip the dough onto a floured work surface, bring together with your hands and divide into four pieces. Flatten each into a disc, wrap in cling film and chill for 1–2 hours, until firm.
3 Preheat the oven to 180C/gas 4 and line two baking sheets.
4 To make the filling, mix the chocolate, pecans, cinnamon and sugar in a mixing bowl. Set aside.
5 On a lightly floured work surface, roll one pastry disc into a neat circle about 2mm thick (leave the other in the fridge for the second batch). Spread with an even layer of jam and scatter with half the filling.
6 Using a long knife or pizza wheel, divide the circle into six wedges or triangles. Roll each triangle into a crescent, starting from the outside and rolling towards the point.
7 Arrange the pastries on the baking sheets, brush with egg and sprinkle with sugar. Bake in the middle of the oven for 20 minutes, until golden. Meanwhile, make the second batch.

RASPBERRY, YOGHURT & POLENTA CAKE

Per serving 243 cals, 15.5g fat (7.8g sat fats), 3g protein, 23.9g carbs, 11.8g sugars

··

RASPBERRY, YOGHURT & POLENTA CAKE

Serves 8 Ⓥ

- 125g butter, softened, plus extra for greasing
- 200g raspberries, plus extra to serve
- 225g flour
- 225g golden caster sugar
- 2 large eggs
- Grated zest and juice of 2 lemons
- 2 tsp baking powder
- 50g polenta
- 125g yoghurt
- 200g icing sugar

1 Preheat the oven to 170C/gas 3. Grease and line a 900g loaf tin. In a bowl, toss the raspberries with 1 tablespoon of flour and set aside.
2 In another bowl, beat the butter and sugar until fluffy, then beat in the eggs. Stir in the lemon zest.
3 Sieve the remaining flour and baking powder. Fold it into the batter with the polenta, then the yoghurt.
4 Spoon a third of the batter into the tin, then half the berries. Repeat with another third of the batter and remaining berries. Top with the rest of the batter. Bake for 60–75 minutes, or until a skewer comes out clean.
5 Leave to cool on a wire rack, then turn out of the tin and leave to cool. Put the icing sugar in a bowl and gradually add lemon juice until thick but runny. Drizzle over the cake and finish with more raspberries.

Per serving 485 cals, 15.6g fat (8.6g sat fats), 6.1g protein, 85.1g carbs, 58.3g sugars

CHOCOLATE & SALTED CARAMEL 'JAMMIE DODGERS'

extract, then stir in the egg yolks, one at a time, mixing thoroughly between each addition.

3 Add the dry ingredients to the mixture, in batches, taking care not to overwork the dough or the biscuits will end up tough, rather than crisp and light.

4 Lightly knead the dough to bring it together into a smooth ball, flatten into a disc, wrap in cling film and chill for 1 hour or until firm.

5 Line two baking sheets with baking paper. On a floured surface, roll out the dough to the thickness of a pound coin. Stamp out your biscuits with a 6cm cookie cutter and arrange on the baking sheets.

6 Reshape any leftover dough into a ball, then roll again and cut out more biscuits. Using a 3cm cutter, stamp out a smaller shape from the middle of half the biscuits. Chill for 15 minutes in the fridge and preheat the oven to 170C/gas 3.

7 Bake the biscuits in batches on the middle shelf of the oven for 12-15 minutes, until crisp. Cool on the baking sheets.

8 To make the buttercream, place the softened butter, 1 tablespoon of the caramel, the icing sugar, melted chocolate and a good pinch of salt in a free-standing mixer and beat until really smooth. Keep this mixture in the bowl of the mixer until you need it - it will set too soon if you put it in a piping bag now.

9 When the biscuits are completely cool, scoop the buttercream into a piping bag fitted with a 1cm plain nozzle. Spoon the remaining caramel into another piping bag, fitted with a smaller (0.6) plain nozzle. Pipe a ring of the buttercream around the outside edge of a whole biscuit and just inside this pipe a thin ring of caramel, leaving space in the centre.

10 Top with a ring-shaped biscuit and pipe more caramel into the hole to fill. Repeat with the rest of the biscuits. Drizzle the melted chocolate across the top of the biscuits and leave to set before eating.

Per serving 301.3 cals, 17.4g fat (8.9g sat fats), 4.3g protein, 33.7g carbs, 25.3g sugars

CHOCOLATE & SALTED CARAMEL 'JAMMIE DODGERS'

Most of us have fond memories of Jammie Dodgers from childhood - which is why we love this wickedly grown-up chocolate version, filled with gooey salted caramel. You'll need two round cookie cutters, one smaller than the other (ideally 6cm and 3cm), to get the best effect.

Makes 24 Ⓥ

- 250g plain flour, plus a little extra for dusting
- 100g ground almonds
- ½ tsp baking powder
- 25g cocoa powder
- 225g butter, softened
- 150g golden caster sugar
- 1 tsp vanilla extract
- 3 medium egg yolks
- 100g 70% dark chocolate, melted, to drizzle

Buttercream filling
- 100g butter, softened
- 397g tin Carnation caramel
- 200g icing sugar
- 50g 70% dark chocolate, melted

1 To make the cookies, combine the flour, ground almonds, baking powder, cocoa and a pinch of salt in a mixing bowl and set aside.

2 Beat the butter and sugar until pale and fluffy. Add the vanilla

GOOSEBERRY FOOL DOUGHNUTS

Makes 12 ⓥ

- 460g strong flour, plus extra for dusting
- 30g golden caster sugar, plus extra to serve
- 5g salt
- Zest of 1 orange
- Zest of 1 lemon, plus extra to serve
- 4 large eggs
- 75ml tepid milk
- 1 tbsp yoghurt
- 7g packet dried yeast
- 60g butter, softened
- 1 litre vegetable oil, plus extra for greasing

Gooseberry jam
- 300g gooseberries
- 150g golden caster sugar
- Juice of 1 lemon

Fool custard
- 50g golden caster sugar
- 3 large egg yolks
- 15g custard powder
- 150ml milk
- 100ml double cream
- 1 vanilla pod, split lengthways, seeds scraped
- 50g double cream
- 500g crème fraîche

GOOSEBERRY FOOL DOUGHNUTS

1 Start by making the gooseberry jam. Put the ingredients in a saucepan and place over a medium heat until jammy, about 15-20 minutes. Leave to cool, then put in a piping bag. Chill until ready to use.
2 To start the fool custard, whisk together the sugar, egg yolks and custard powder until super-smooth.
3 Put the milk, cream and vanilla pod and seeds in a pan and bring to the boil. Off the heat, slowly pour a third over the custard mixture and whisk until smooth, discarding the pod. Whisk in the remaining two-thirds.
4 Return to the heat and continue to cook, until the mixture is bubbling rapidly and thickened; whisk continuously during this process to prevent it catching.
5 Push through a fine sieve into a plastic container. Seal the surface with cling film, to prevent a skin, and

chill for 2-3 hours. (You can make up to this step a couple of days ahead.)
6 For the batter, put the flour, sugar, salt and zests into a mixing bowl. Combine the eggs, milk, yoghurt and yeast, and add to the bowl. Mix with a spoon for about 5 minutes, then add the butter and mix for another 5 minutes, until elastic and shiny. Form into a ball and put in a flour-dusted bowl. Cover with cling film. Leave to rise for 2 hours.
7 Divide into 12, put on an oiled baking sheet, then cover and leave until doubled in size. Heat the oil in a large, deep pan to 170C or until a bread cube turns golden in 30 seconds when added.

8 Carefully add 2-3 doughnuts at a time and cook for 6-7 minutes, rotating every minute or so with metal tongs until deep golden brown. Drain on kitchen roll and allow the doughnuts to cool before filling.
9 To finish the custard, beat until it's smooth. In a separate bowl, whisk the cream and crème fraîche to stiff peaks and fold this into the custard.
10 Spoon the jam into one piping bag and the custard into another. Make a hole in each doughnut, pipe in the jam, then the custard. Combine the extra sugar and lemon zest, then roll your finished doughnuts in them.
Per serving 588 cals, 37.8g fat (19.2g sat fats), 10.4g protein, 55.4g carbs, 25.7g sugars

FRUIT & NUT FLAPJACKS

FRUIT & NUT FLAPJACKS
Makes 12 Ⓥ

- 175g butter
- 175g golden syrup
- 175g muscovado sugar
- 300g porridge oats
- 100g walnuts, chopped
- 50g mixed dried fruit (such as raisins, sultanas and cherries)
- 2 tbsp golden linseed

1 Preheat the oven to 150C/gas 2. Line a 20cm-square baking tin with baking paper. Place the butter, golden syrup and sugar in a medium saucepan over a low heat and stir occasionally, until the sugar has dissolved and the butter has melted. **2** Remove the pan from the heat and stir in the oats, nuts, dried fruit and linseed. Spoon the mixture into the tin, then flatten with a wooden spoon. Bake for 35-40 minutes,

then remove from the oven and leave to cool for 15 minutes, or until the flapjacks have firmed up. **3** Turn out onto a chopping board and cut into squares. Serve warm or at room temperature.
Per serving 380 cals, 20.8g fat (8.2g sat fats), 4.7g protein, 44g carbs, 29.8g sugars

....

GINGER & WALNUT CAKE
Serves 10-12 Ⓥ

- 250g unsalted butter, plus extra for greasing
- 200g dark brown sugar
- 200g black treacle
- 3 eggs, beaten
- A thumb-size piece of ginger, peeled and grated
- 250g plain flour
- 1 tsp bicarbonate of soda
- 1 tsp mixed spice
- 300g plain yoghurt

Praline
- Unsalted butter, for greasing
- 250g walnuts, plus extra to decorate
- 250g golden caster sugar

Buttercream
- 250g unsalted butter, softened
- 240g cream cheese
- 450g icing sugar, sifted

1 Preheat the oven to 180C/gas 4. Grease two 20cm loose-bottomed cake tins and line the bases with baking paper. Place the butter, sugar and treacle in a pan and heat gently until melted. Take off the heat then stir in the eggs and the grated ginger. **2** Place the flour, bicarb of soda and spice in a large bowl and blend well. Stir in the butter mixture until blended, then mix in the yoghurt. Divide the mixture between the tins. **3** Bake for 45-50 minutes, until a skewer comes out clean. Leave to cool in the tin for 1 hour, then turn out onto a wire rack. **4** For the praline, lightly toast the walnuts in a pan over a low heat, until golden. Grease a piece of baking paper with butter and set aside. **5** Place the sugar in a pan and melt over a low heat until a dark caramel colour. Place the nuts on the baking sheet and carefully pour over the caramel. Leave until cold and set, then blitz briefly in a food processor until it breaks into smallish pieces. **6** To make the buttercream, beat the butter and cream cheese until smooth, then mix in the icing sugar. **7** With a serrated knife, slice off the dome from both cakes, so they're flat. Cut each cake in half. Set the top half of one cake on a board. Spread an even layer of the buttercream on top. **8** Place the bottom half of the cake, base upwards, on top. Repeat with buttercream and cake layers, finishing with the bottom of the second cake, base-side up, on top. **9** Cover the cake with more buttercream, then decorate with the praline pieces and extra walnuts. Chill in the fridge until ready to serve.
Per serving 715 cals, 42.5g fat (19.8g sat fats), 7.1g protein, 81.5g carbs, 69.1g sugars

MULTI-TASKING MADE EASY

Cooking would be such a cinch with a full arsenal of kitchen appliances, but who has the space for a multitude of machines?

Magimix has come up with a solution in its new Pâtissier Multifunction appliance, which transforms from a stand mixer to a fully equipped, three-bowl food processor. You can blend soups and smoothies, slice, grate and chop, knead bread dough, whisk egg whites and much more, all using the one clever appliance.

Quick, quiet and efficient, the Pâtissier Multifunction combines the blending power of a food processor with all the handy tools required for perfect baking. Available in retailers nationwide, it comes in a range of five distinctive colours: vanille, framboise, red, black and satin. Skillful and stylish, this is the ultimate dream machine for any cook.

BUTTERMILK & BANANA MUFFINS

BUTTERMILK & BANANA MUFFINS

These are little rays of sunshine, fluffy, banana-rich muffins, specked with golden sultanas.

Makes 12 ⓥ

- 200g wholemeal self-raising flour
- 80g porridge oats
- 100g golden caster sugar
- 2 tsp baking powder
- ½ tsp salt
- 1 large egg
- 75ml vegetable oil
- 175ml buttermilk
- 250g ripe bananas, mashed
- 40g golden sultanas

1 Preheat the oven to 200C/gas 6. In a bowl, combine the flour, oats, sugar, baking powder and salt. In a bowl, beat the egg with an electric whisk. Stir in the oil and buttermilk.
2 Tip in the mashed bananas, the flour mixture and most of the sultanas, then fold to combine.
3 Line a 12-hole muffin tin with paper cases and divide the batter between them, then scatter with the reserved sultanas. Bake in the middle of the oven for 18-20 minutes, until golden.

Per serving 208 cals, 7.8g fat (1g sat fats), 4.3g protein, 31.4g carbs, 16.5g sugars

RHUBARB & POLENTA CAKE

RHUBARB & POLENTA CAKE
Serves 8 ⓥ

- 400g rhubarb, cut into 4cm pieces
- 150g sugar, plus 1 tbsp extra
- 150g ground almonds
- 100g quick-cook polenta
- 50g plain flour
- 1 tsp baking powder
- 150g greek yoghurt
- 4 eggs, beaten
- Zest and juice of 1 orange, plus 1 orange slice, cut into triangles

1 Preheat the oven to 180C/gas 4. Line a 20 x 5cm cake tin. Toss the rhubarb in the extra sugar and bake on a tray for 15 minutes, until tender. **2** In a bowl, combine the almonds, polenta, flour, baking powder and the rest of the sugar, then stir in the yoghurt, eggs and orange zest and juice. Place half of the rhubarb in the bottom of the tin and spoon over the batter. Arrange the orange triangles and the rest of the rhubarb on top. **3** Bake for 45 minutes, or until a skewer inserted into the centre comes out clean. Remove from the tin and cool on a rack before serving.
Per serving 285 cals, 11.6g fat (1.6g sat fats), 8.4g protein, 37.6g carbs, 22.2g sugars

#birramoretti

DRINKS

BIRRA MORETTI

for the facts
drinkaware.co.uk

PURE GOOSEBERRY CORDIAL

ESSEX COCKTAIL

ICED CANTALOUPE SMOOTHIE

For a bit of extra zing, add some grated lime zest or the juice of half a lime to the mix

Serves 1 (GF) (V)

- 200g cantaloupe melon flesh
- 100ml plain yoghurt
- Wedges of melon to garnish (optional)

1 Fill a tall glass with crushed ice. Using a food processor, blend the melon and yoghurt until smooth.
2 Pour over the crushed ice and serve immediately, garnished with an extra melon wedge, if desired.

Per serving 97 cals, 0.2g fat (0g sat fats), 7.1g protein, 16.9g carbs, 16.9g sugars

PURE GOOSEBERRY CORDIAL

Makes 1.5 litres (DF) (GF) (V) (VG)

- 2kg gooseberries
- 1kg (approximately) golden caster sugar
- Lemon wedges, to serve

1 Put the berries and sugar in a large pan with 500ml water and gently mash the fruit with a masher. Bring to the boil, stirring, then simmer for 20-30 minutes. until thickened.
2 Strain through a fine sieve and taste, to see if it needs more sugar. Pour through a large piece of muslin suspended over a large bowl.
3 Leave for a good few hours, or overnight, until all the liquid has drained through. Discard the pulp and pour into sterilised bottles. Keep in the fridge for up to three months.

Per 100ml 24 cals, 0g fat (0g sat fats), 0.1g protein, 6.2g carbs, 6.2g sugars

ESSEX COCKTAIL

Serves 1 (DF) (V) (VG)

- 60ml Bombay Sapphire Gin
- 25ml ginger syrup (see note)
- 20ml freshly squeezed lemon juice (about 1 lemon), plus a little extra for the rim of the glass
- Maldon sea salt
- Light beer or lager, such as Essex Felstar Peckin' Order, chilled

1 Put the gin, ginger syrup and lemon juice in a blender with a large handful of cubed ice, then blitz.
2 Rub the rim of a handled beer glass with lemon juice, invert the glass, then press into a plate of sea salt.
3 Pour the cocktail into the glass, top up with lager and serve.

Note Ginger syrup is available online from verdecoffee.com.

Per serving 228 cals, 0.2g fat (0.1g sat fats), 0.4g protein, 20.2g carbs, 19.4g sugars

Pairing drinks with food extends to much more than wine. A classic crisp lager, such as Birra Moretti, perfectly complements all sorts of dishes, from a classic spaghetti vongole to a simple margherita pizza. But you can even use it in cooking as you would with vino. Make a light beer batter for fish using Birra Moretti, or add rich, amber Moretti La Rossa to a beef stew for extra flavour depth.

MANGO & COCONUT SLURPY
Serves 4 (DF)(GF)(V)

- 500g cubed mango flesh
- 4 tbsp chopped mint
- 2 tbsp honey
- 400ml light coconut milk
- 2 tbsp flaxseeds

1 Place all the ingredients in a blender along with 250ml of ice-cold water. Blend until thick, then pour into four chilled glasses and scatter the flaxseeds on top.
Per serving 163 cals, 9.1g fat (5.6g sat fats), 2.8g protein, 17.2g carbs, 9.5g sugars

BOULEVARDIER
Serves 1 (DF)(GF)(V)(VG)

- 30ml bourbon
- 30ml Martini Bitter
- 30ml Martini Rosso
- A twist or strip of orange peel and sour cherries, to garnish

1 Pour the bourbon and both Martinis into a rocks glass over ice cubes. Stir 3-4 times, then garnish with the orange peel and sour cherries.
Per serving 133cals, 0g fat (0g sat fats), 0.1g protein, 7.7g carbs, 7.7g sugars

EARL GREY & ORANGE ICED TEA
Makes 1.6 litres (DF)(GF)(V)(VG)

- 3 tbsp golden caster sugar
- 4 earl grey tea bags
- 6 sprigs of mint, plus extra
- 300ml orange juice
- Orange slices, to garnish

1 In a pan, bring 1 litre of water to the boil, then add the sugar. Take off the heat; pop in the tea bags and mint.
2 Cover and infuse for 10 minutes. Strain and leave to cool. Pour into a pitcher of ice with the orange juice. Garnish with the orange slices and extra mint sprigs.
Per serving 20 cals, 0g fat (0g sat fats), 0.1g protein, 5.3g carbs, 5.3g sugars

FLORA SANGRIA

FLORA SANGRIA
Top tip: freeze grapes or edible flowers (or both) in ice cubes for a really decorative drink.
Makes 1 litre (DF)(GF)(V)(VG)

- 250ml St Germain
- 75cl bottle of dry white wine
- 1 small pear, chopped or sliced
- A handful of redcurrants
- 1 clementine, sliced into wheels
- 1 lemon, sliced into wheels

1 Mix all the ingredients together and serve over ice in either a carafe or sangria-style glasses.
Per serving 125 cals, 0g fat (0g sat fats), 0.1g protein, 6.6g carbs, 6.6g sugars

HOT CUBAN COFFEE COCKTAIL
Serves 1 (GF)(V)

- 50ml Bacardi Gold Rum
- 15ml agave nectar
- 15ml amaretto
- Shot of espresso
- Coconut cream and 70% dark chocolate, to serve

1 Add the rum, agave, amaretto and coffee to a pan and gently heat. Pour into a coffee glass and top with coconut cream. Grate over the dark chocolate to serve.
Per serving 196 cals, 0g fat (0g sat fats), 0.1g protein, 15.5g carbs, 13.6g sugars

CLOCKWISE FROM TOP LEFT:
HOT CUBAN COFFEE COCKTAIL; MANGO
& COCONUT SLURPY; BOULEVARDIER;
EARL GREY & ORANGE ICED TEA

YOGHURT, HONEY &
STRAWBERRY SMOOTHIE

STRAWBERRY &
MINT LEMONADE

CLEMENTINE CRUSH

IMMUNE-BOOSTER JUICE

YOGHURT, HONEY & STRAWBERRY SMOOTHIE
Serves 4 (GF) (V)
- 500g strawberries
- 2 ripe bananas, peeled
- 300g fat-free plain yoghurt
- 2 tbsp runny honey

1 Combine all the ingredients in a blender. Blitz until smooth and pour into four glasses to serve.
Per serving 125 cals, 0.3g fat (0.1g sat fats), 6g protein, 25.5g carbs, 24.3g sugars

STRAWBERRY & MINT LEMONADE
Serves 12 (Makes 600ml concentrate) (DF) (GF) (V) (VG)
- 250g golden caster sugar
- Zest and juice of 5 lemons
- 1 large bunch of mint, leaves picked, reserving a few sprigs
- 200g strawberries, hulled, plus 8, quartered, to serve
- Chilled sparkling water, to top up

1 Combine the sugar, zest and 400ml water in a pan over a medium heat and stir until the sugar dissolves. Simmer for 5 minutes, until reduced.
2 In a food processor, blitz the mint, berries and lemon juice together, add the sugar syrup, leave for 5 minutes, then strain. Allow to cool, then chill.
3 To serve, pour 75ml of concentrate into a glass over ice, top up with about 150ml sparkling water, then garnish with mint and strawberries.
Per serving 93 cals, 0.1g fat (0g sat fats), 0.5g protein, 24.2g carbs, 24g sugars

CLEMENTINE CRUSH
Serves 2 (DF) (GF) (V) (VG)
- 100ml clementine juice
- 100ml pomegranate juice
- 50ml vodka
- Pomegranate seeds, to serve

1 Combine the liquids in a cocktail shaker with a handful of ice. Shake well. Strain into glasses of crushed ice and top with pomegranate seeds.

WATERMELON & BASIL JUICE

Per serving 96 cals, 0g fat (0g sat fats), 0.4g protein, 9.9g carbs, 9.9g sugars

IMMUNE-BOOSTER JUICE
Packed with folate and vitamin C to help you fight fatigue.
Serves 2 (DF) (GF) (V) (VG)
- 1 cantaloupe melon, peeled, deseeded and cut into cubes
- 2 beetroots, cut into large cubes
- 6 carrots, cut into large cubes
- 3 oranges, peeled and diced

1 Run all the ingredients through a juicer. Serve in a large jug with ice.
Per serving 75 cals, 0.2g fat (0g sat fats), 1.6g protein, 17.8g carbs, 17.8g sugars

WATERMELON & BASIL JUICE
Makes 1.5 litres (DF) (GF) (V)
- 1 small watermelon, peeled, deseeded and chopped
- 1 tbsp finely chopped basil leaves
- 1 tbsp honey
- 200ml sparkling water
- Apple slices, to garnish (optional)

1 Freeze the watermelon on a baking sheet for at least 1 hour.
2 Blitz the frozen melon in a food processor along with the basil, honey and sparkling water, until smooth. Garnish with apple slices, then serve.
Per serving 30 cals, 0.3g fat (0.1g sat fats), 0.4g protein, 7.2g carbs, 7.1g sugars

DISCOVER THE AUTHENTIC TASTE OF ITALY

Italians do classics well and their beer is no exception. Since 1859, when Luigi Moretti founded his brewery in the northeastern town of Udine, Birra Moretti has continued to be made according to its authentic recipe, and using only the finest ingredients.

A special type of hop provides a unique aroma and enhances the perfectly poised bitterness with delicate malt notes, to make a full-bodied and well-balanced lager. This taste profile means Birra Moretti lends itself perfectly to being enjoyed on its own or with a wide variety of food.

The culture and cuisine of Italy is a firm favourite in Britain, and Birra Moretti, through its annual tour, is championing the best of Italian street food in the UK – perfectly complemented by Birra Moretti.

Italian food varies widely amongst the 20 different regions in Italy, with each having particular dishes or ingredients that they call their own. For each leg of the tour, food is on offer that showcases these regions and all the fantastic food they have to offer.

Birra Moretti will visit a wide range of national events in 2016, including Jamie Oliver's Big Feastival, so look out for it, and enjoy an authentic tour of Italy right here in the UK. Buon Appetito!

GINGER, MINT & CHILLI INFUSION

GINGER, MINT & CHILLI INFUSION
Serves 2 (DF) (GF) (V) (VG)

This will liven up your day - it's like dynamite in a cup!

- 5cm piece of fresh ginger, peeled and thinly sliced
- ½ bunch of mint, leaves only
- 5-6 thin slices of red chilli (not bird's-eye, unless you like things super-fiery!), deseeded if you prefer a milder heat.

1 Divide all of the ingredients between 2 cups, and cover with boiling water. Drink and enjoy. The chilli will get stronger as the drink stands, so take it out when (or if!) you like.
Per serving 4 cals, 0.1g fat (0g sat fats), 0.3g protein, 0.7g carbs, 0.4g sugars

TORMENTA NEGRA
(Pictured on p157)

Spanish for 'black storm', this is a take on the classic dark and stormy cocktail.
Serves 1 (DF) (V) (VG)

- 10-15ml lime juice, plus ½ lime, to garnish
- 50ml Bacardi Carta Negra rum
- 3 dashes of Angostura bitters
- 100ml ginger beer
- A sprig of mint, to garnish

1 Fill a highball glass with ice, squeeze in the lime juice and add the rum, bitters and ginger beer, then stir. Garnish with the lime and mint.
Per serving 168 cals, 0g fat (0g sat fats), 0.1g protein, 14.5g carbs, 14.5g sugars

COCOA-VANILLA SMOOTHIE

ORECCHIETTE WITH PRAWNS & BROAD BEANS

Recipe by David Toscano, of pop-up restaurant Cin Cin in East Sussex
Serves 6

- Olive oil
- 1 onion, peeled and thinly sliced
- 1 garlic clove, peeled and crushed
- 1 chilli, thinly sliced
- 100g fresh broad beans
- 500g raw prawns, peeled and deveined
- 100ml white wine
- 100ml fish stock
- 250g orecchiette pasta
- A handful of torn mint leaves

1 Heat 2 tablespoons of olive oil over a medium heat and gently fry the onion for 5 minutes. Add the garlic and chilli and sauté for few more minutes.
2 Blanch the broad beans in boiling water for 5 minutes, drain, then add to the pan with the prawns for 3 minutes more.
3 Season, then add the wine and cook for 3 minutes, until the wine has evaporated. Pour in the stock and cook for another 3 minutes.
4 While the sauce is simmering, cook the orecchiette in boiling salted water until al dente.
5 Drain the pasta, reserving some of the cooking water. Add this to the sauce to loosen, if you think it needs it.
6 Tip the pasta to pan of sauce and toss to combine. Divide between plates, scatter over the mint and serve with a drizzle of olive oil.

COCOA-VANILLA SMOOTHIE

Serves 1 (v)

- 200g plain yoghurt
- 150g semi-skimmed milk
- 1 wholewheat Weetabix or similar cereal biscuit
- A few drops of vanilla bean extract
- 1 tsp cocoa powder, plus extra to dust

1 Blend all of the ingredients in a food processor until creamy and smooth. Pour into a glass or bottle and serve with an extra dusting of cocoa powder on top.

Per serving 268 cals, 3.8g fat (2.1g sat fats), 19.7g protein, 39.6g carbs, 25g sugars

ELDERFLOWER & CUCUMBER SPRITZER

(Not pictured)
Makes 600ml (DF) (GF) (v) (VG)

- 1 cucumber, cut into 2cm chunks
- 200ml clear apple juice
- 200ml elderflower cordial
- 8-12 sprigs of mint
- About 1 litre chilled soda water

1 In a blender, blitz the cucumber, apple juice and cordial. Strain through a sieve into a bowl or jug. Add 1-2 tablespoons of the pulp; discard the rest. Chill until needed.
2 To serve, fill glasses with a few ice cubes and 2-3 mint sprigs. Fill the glasses halfway with your spritzer mixture, then top up with chilled soda water and serve.

Per serving 10 cals, 0g fat (0g sat fats), 0.2g protein, 2.2g carbs, 2.2g sugars

Pickle as it should be...

Give your sandwich the partner it deserves with our new, naturally delicious and all grown up Proper Pickles.

Choose between Beetroot, Pickled Onion, traditional Chunky or traditional Finely Chopped; they're packed full of flavour and the perfect amount of punch for your palate.

It's pickle as it should be, *it's Proper Pickle.*

SINCE 1979

English Provender

www.englishprovender.com

SAUCES & EXTRAS

The English
Provender Co.

SPICED AUBERGINE DIP

SPICY PICKLED RUNNER BEANS

HONEY CASHEW BUTTER

SPICED AUBERGINE DIP

Makes 600g (DF) (V) (VG)

- 2 large aubergines
- 1 tbsp vegetable oil
- 2 onions, peeled and finely chopped
- 4 garlic cloves, peeled and crushed
- 2 tsp grated ginger
- 1–2 green chillies, finely sliced
- 3 tomatoes, chopped, plus extra slices to garnish
- 2 tbsp curry powder
- 8 tbsp chopped coriander leaves
- Oven-baked corn tortillas, sliced, to serve

1 Preheat the oven to 220C/gas 7. Prick the aubergines all over with a fork, then place on a roasting tray. Roast for 50-60 minutes, or until the skin blackens and chars and the flesh can be easily pierced with a spoon. Allow to cool to room temperature. **2** Cut the cooled aubergines in half, scoop the flesh into a food processor and pulse until smooth. Set aside. **3** Heat the oil in a large frying pan. Add the onion and sauté for 5–6 minutes, until softened. Add the garlic, ginger and chilli, then stir-fry for 1–2 minutes. Stir in the tomatoes and curry powder and cook for 12-15 minutes, until softened. **4** Stir in the reserved aubergine and cook the mixture, stirring, for 3-4 minutes. Stir in the coriander leaves, then take the pan off the heat. Spoon the dip into a serving bowl, garnish with the extra tomato slices and serve with the warm tortilla chips.

Per 100g 50 cals, 2.1g fat (0.3g sat fats), 1.7g protein, 6.5g carbs, 4.7g sugars

SPICY PICKLED RUNNER BEANS

Label your pickles and leave them for at least 2-3 weeks to mellow before eating them.

Makes 2 x 400ml jars (DF) (GF) (V) (VG)

- 500g runner beans, sliced
- 500ml cider vinegar
- 2 tsp sugar
- 2 tsp mustard seeds
- 12 black peppercorns
- 2 bay leaves
- 2 yellow chillies, sliced into rounds (see note)

1 Place the beans into sterilised jam jars. Put the other ingredients in a saucepan with 250ml water and 2 teaspoons sea salt and place over a medium heat. Bring to the boil and leave to simmer for 5 minutes. **2** Carefully pour the pickling liquid into the jam jars and put the lids on securely before storing them in a cool, dark place to mellow. **Note** Citrusy yellow chillies are originally from Peru. You can find them at good supermarkets or at southdevonchillifarm.co.uk.

Per 100g 25 cals, 0.4g fat (0.1g sat fats), 1.1g protein, 2.9g carbs, 2.5g sugars

HONEY CASHEW BUTTER

Makes about 250g (DF) (GF) (V)

- 250g cashew nuts
- 1 tbsp honey, or to taste

1 Preheat your oven to 170C/gas 3. Spread the nuts on a baking tray and roast for 8-10 minutes, until lightly golden. Leave to cool completely. **2** Tip the nuts into a food processor and blitz for 10 minutes, or until smooth and buttery. **3** Transfer the spread to a bowl, add the honey (enough to suit your own taste), and mix well. This is great in a smoothie or on sourdough toast.

Per tbsp 87 cals, 6.9g fat (1.4g sat fats), 2.5g protein, 3.6g carbs, 1.7g sugars

Sauces can elevate the simplest ingredients, but for those moments when you don't have time to make one from scratch, a good chutney can be a super staple. Try a tomato-based chutney as a speedy salsa for fajitas, or a pepper-based one to liven up a cheese and broccoli quiche – just spoon over the pastry before you pour in your filling. Enrich your chilli con carne by stirring through 2 tablespoons of tomato chutney towards the end of cooking. It's a handy little helper!

ROASTED SHALLOT SAUCE

SARDINE & TOMATO PATE

TARRAGON MAYO

ROASTED SHALLOT SAUCE

This rich, sweet sauce is lovely served with chicken or game.

Serves 4

- 16 shallots, halved if large
- 1 large celery stalk, quartered
- 1 large carrot, quartered
- 1 tbsp olive oil
- ½ garlic bulb
- 200ml red wine
- 750ml just-boiled chicken or game stock
- 50g butter, softened
- 1 tbsp plain flour
- 200g vacuum-packed chestnuts
- 2 rosemary sprigs
- 1 tsp dijon mustard

1 Preheat the oven to 180C/gas 4. Put the shallots, celery and carrot in a snug roasting tray, season and drizzle with the oil.
2 Wrap the garlic in tinfoil and add to the tray. Roast for 45 minutes, or until the veg is soft and golden. Place the vegetables, except the garlic, in a pan, add the wine and bring to the boil. Bubble until it's almost evaporated, then add the stock.
3 Combine the butter and flour, and whisk in. Bring the sauce to the boil, add the chestnuts, 1 rosemary sprig

and the mustard. Squeeze the garlic from its skin and whisk it in.
4 Cook for 10 minutes, or until it has reduced and thickened. Pick out any big pieces of veg, then garnish with the remaining rosemary.

Per tbsp 632 cals, 32.2 fat (14.3g sat fats), 16.6g protein, 55.4g carbs, 15.9g sugars

....

SARDINE & TOMATO PATE

Serves 4-6

- 2 x 120g tins sardines in tomato sauce
- 2 tomatoes, deseeded and chopped
- 2 tbsp finely chopped chives
- 1 garlic clove, peeled and crushed
- Finely grated zest and juice of 1 lemon
- 170g pack light soft cheese with garlic and herbs
- 1 tsp pink peppercorns in brine, drained and roughly crushed
- 2 tbsp cornichons, finely chopped
- Rye crispbread, wholemeal melba toast, gem lettuce or chicory leaves and crudités, to serve

1 Place all of the ingredients, except for the pink peppercorns

and cornichons, into a mini food processor or chopper. Blitz for about 1 minute, or until you have a texture you like – it's great either chunky or smooth.
2 Season, stir in the peppercorns and cornichons, then transfer the pâté to ramekins. Cover and chill in the fridge until you are ready to eat.
3 Spread on crispbread or toast, spoon into lettuce or chicory leaves, or serve with crudités on the side.

Per serving 144 cals, 7.2 fat (2.5g sat fats), 15.6g protein, 5.5g carbs, 5.3g sugars

....

TARRAGON MAYO

Makes 400ml (DF) (V)

- 2 cooked egg yolks (they should still be runny, not set)
- 1 tsp mustard
- 300ml olive or rapeseed oil
- Juice of ½ lemon
- 1 tbsp chopped tarragon

1 Mash together the egg yolks and mustard. Very slowly whisk in the oil, until thickened. Add a squeeze of lemon juice to loosen. Season and stir through the tarragon.

Per tbsp 115 cals, 12.6 fat (1g sat fats), 0.3g protein, 0g carbs, 0g sugars

HUNGER'S LITTLE HELPER

Whether you want to whip up a quick bite or boost your baking, a good-quality chutney will rev up the flavour and save you time. The English Provender Co.'s popular Caramelised Red Onion Chutney is delicious with just about everything, from quiches to sarnies. Try these simple ideas with Caramelised Red Onion Chutney.

- For cheesy onion mash:
  Add a handful of grated cheese and a couple of tablespoons of onion chutney, to the mashed potato. Delicious served with pork chops or sausages.
- For delicious cheese on toast:
  Lightly toast one side of the bread, turn over and spread with the caramelized onion chutney, then top with grated cheese. Return to the grill and cook until bubbling and golden, then serve with a crisp green salad.
- For a posh burger:
  Add a couple of tablespoons of chutney to minced beef, shape into burgers and grill. Serve in brioche burger buns with rocket leaves and a little more chutney.
- For caramelised onion macaroni cheese:
  Stir in a couple of tablespoons of the chutney to your cheese sauce.
- For simple canapés:
  Place a slice of blue cheese on top of some toasted bread, add a spoonful of chutney to each and garnish with chopped chives.

For more recipe ideas, visit www.englishprovender.com or see our recipe far right

The English Provender Co.

CRANBERRY & CHILLI JAM

CRANBERRY & CHILLI JAM
Makes 700g (DF) (GF) (V) (VG)
- 2 red onions, finely sliced
- 4 garlic cloves, finely chopped
- 3-4 long red chillies, deseeded and finely sliced
- Olive oil
- 500g fresh cranberries
- 150g sugar
- 40ml red wine vinegar

1 Place the onions, garlic and chillies in a large pan over a low heat. Add a little oil and sweat down until the onions are soft but not coloured, about 8-10 minutes.
2 Add the cranberries, sugar, vinegar and 50ml water. Simmer for 15-20 minutes, until the berries are breaking down but just holding their shape.
3 Gently mash and cook for a further 15 minutes, until thickened. Season with salt, pepper and a drizzle of oil. Allow the jam to cool then spoon into sterilised jars. It keeps for 1 week.
Per tbsp 30 cals, 0.2 fat (0g sat fats), 0.4g protein, 6.8g carbs, 6.4g sugars

RED CHILLI SALSA
(not pictured)
Serves 4 (DF) (GF) (V) (VG)
- 2 red chillies, deseeded and finely chopped
- 2 red onions, peeled and finely chopped
- 2 tomatoes, deseeded and finely chopped
- 1 tbsp coriander stalks, chopped
- Juice of 4 limes
- 100ml olive oil

1 Place all the ingredients in a bowl and mix well to combine, then

VANILLA EXTRACT

season with salt and pepper. This is ideal served with grilled meats.

Per serving 254 cals, 25.2 fat (3.6g sat fats), 1.1g protein, 5.9g carbs, 4.8g sugars

VANILLA EXTRACT

Why buy premade essences, (some of which contain added sugar) when it's so easy to make your own? This is also a nifty homemade gift for any cook.

Makes 50ml (DF) (GF) (V) (VG)

- 1 vanilla pod, split lengthways
- 50ml bottle of rum or vodka

1 Remove a little alcohol from the bottle, and stuff both halves of the pod inside. Pop on the lid and leave to steep for at least 3 weeks .

Per tsp 10.7 cals, 0g fat (0g sat fats), 0g protein, 0g carbs, 0g sugars

TANGY BEETROOT DIP

(pictured on p167)

Makes 350g (GF) (V)

- 250g cooked beetroot
- ½ small garlic clove, peeled
- Olive oil
- 100g low-fat yoghurt

1 Blitz the beetroot and garlic in a food processor or blender until just combined.
2 Add a drizzle of oil and the yoghurt, then blitz again until you have a nice chunky dip. Season and finish with a drizzle of olive oil.

Per tbsp 10 cals, 0.3 fat (0g sat fats), 0.5g protein, 1.4g carbs, 1.3g sugars

ONION CHUTNEY & GOATS' CHEESE SAUSAGE ROLLS

- 375g ready-rolled puff pastry
- Plain flour, for dusting
- 450g pork sausage meat
- 2 tbsp freshly chopped sage
- 175g The English Provender Co. Caramelised Red Onion Chutney
- 100g hard goats' cheese, grated
- 1 egg, beaten
- 2 tsp poppy seeds

Preheat the oven to 220C/gas 7. On a floured surface, unroll the pastry and halve lengthways. Spoon the chutney over the base of each piece, leaving a 2.5cm border. Sprinkle over 75g of the cheese. Combine the sausage meat and sage in a bowl, divide in two and, with wet hands, form each into a skinny sausage the same length as the pastry. Place one in the middle of each pastry piece, brush one long edge with egg and roll up, so the pastry overlaps. Cut each into six rolls. Transfer to a non-stick baking sheet, brush with egg and sprinkle with poppy seeds and the remaining cheese. Bake for 20 mins, or until cooked and golden.

The English Provender Co.

INDEX

EDITOR	Andy Harris
MANAGING EDITOR	Paul Dring
DEPUTY EDITOR	Emma Ventura
ART DIRECTOR	Andrew Jackson
DEPUTY ART DIRECTOR	Helen Little
FOOD EDITOR	Clare Knivett
SUB-EDITOR	Claire Nelson
EDITORIAL ASSISTANT	Heather Taylor
LICENSING & SYNDICATION	Mandie Howard
SUBSCRIPTIONS MANAGER	Gemma Heavens
EDITOR AT LARGE	Jamie Oliver

RECIPES

Omar Allibhoy, Bacardi, Richard Bertinet, Martin Boetz, The Chiappa Sisters, Charlie Clapp, Gennaro Contaldo, Paul Cunningham, Rodney Dunn, Emily Ezekiel, Marina Filippelli, Giuseppe Gallo, Hangfire Smokehouse, Andy Harris, Lizzie Harris, Alice Hart, Georgina Hayden, Mark Hix, Cara Hobday, Robbin Holmgren, Jane Hornby, Dan Jones, Jodene Jordan, Amber Locke, Ed Loftus, Mama's Jerk Station, Christina Mackenzie, Elspeth Meston, Martin Morales, Jools Oliver, Mr Peng, Martin Poole, Stephane Reynaud, Annie Rigg, Maddie Rix, Ginny Rolfe, Carlo Scotto, Maja Smend, Philippa Spence, Sam Stowell, Susie Theodorou, Sarah Tildesley, Will Torrent, Sunil Vijayaker, Thao Vilayvong

PHOTOGRAPHY

Simon Bajada, Laura Edwards, Tara Fisher, Jonathan Gregson, Will Heap, Emma Lee, David Loftus, Gareth Morgans, David Munns, Myles New, Martin Poole, Matt Russell, Anders Schønneman, Toby Scott, Maja Smend, Sam Stowell, Rob Streeter, Kate Whittaker

ADVERTISING

Rob Biagioni, John Brown Media, 020 7565 3206
Gayle Curtis, John Brown Media, 020 7565 3313

JAMIE OLIVER LTD

CEO	Paul Hunt
CEO JAMIE OLIVER MEDIA	Tara Donovan
HEAD OF LEGAL	Giovanna Milia

SUBSCRIPTIONS

Jamie Magazine, Regal Place, Maxwell Road, London SW6 2HD.
0800 953 9800 (or +44 20 7814 5064 from outside the UK), jamiemagazine@hhs.co.uk

Distribution by COMAG, Unit 3, Tavistock Road, West Drayton, Middlesex UB7 7QE. 01895 433600

Jamie magazine is published by Jamie Magazine Ltd. Registered Office 19–21 Nile Street, London N1 7LL, UK; 020 3375 5601. Jamie is a registered trademark. Copyright 2014 Jamie Magazine Ltd.

Any reproduction without permission is prohibited. Jamie magazine contains editorial content from external contributors, which does not necessarily reflect the views of Jamie Magazine Ltd.

Jamie magazine does not accept or respond to unsolicited manuscripts and photographs. The publishers do not accept responsibility for errors in advertisements or third-party offers. Jamie magazine is printed in the UK by Southernprint Ltd. Print management & reprographic services by John Brown.

Member of the Audit Bureau of Circulations

SPECIAL OFFER

GREAT REASONS TO SUBSCRIBE

- Save 30% on the cover price
- Get a free copy of *Everyday Super Food* (rrp £30)*
- 75+ recipes in every issue, including exclusive new recipes from Jamie Oliver

- All recipes road-tested in the Jamie Oliver kitchens, to make sure they work time after time
- A great gift for a foodie friend. They don't just get one present, they get 10 throughout the year!

Call us now on
0800 953 9800
and quote code YB7

(Lines open 8am–8pm Mon–Fri; 9am–1pm Sat)

Order online at
jamiemagazine.com/YB7

USEFUL INFO

WEIGHT

Imperial	Metric
1 oz	28g
1 lb	450g

LIQUID

1 teaspoon	5ml
1 dessertspoon	12ml
1 tablespoon	15ml
1 shot	25ml
1 small wine glass	125ml
1 large wine glass	250ml
1 fl oz	30ml
1 pint	568ml
1 glug	about 20ml

CUP MEASURES

	US	AUS
1 cup sugar	200g	220g
1 cup flour	115g	125g
1 cup liquid	240ml	250ml

OVEN TEMPERATURES

Celsius	Fahrenheit	Gas Mark
110C	225F	¼
130C	250F	½
140C	275F	1
150C	300F	2
170C	325F	3
180C	350F	4
190C	375F	5
200C	400F	6
220C	425F	7
230C	450F	8

For fan-assisted ovens, reduce temperatures by 10–20C

INGREDIENTS

- We use Freedom Foods certified, free-range, organic or higher-welfare pork and chicken and their by-products, including large eggs with an average weight of 60g.
- Whenever possible, we look for sustainably managed fish, with an MSC or Freedom Foods mark.
- We use either beef gelatine or vegetarian setting agents, such as agar agar, and adjust for liquid quantity used in recipe according to packet instructions.
- Unless otherwise indicated, all herbs in recipes are fresh; we season with sea salt and freshly ground black pepper; vegetables
and fruits are washed and trimmed; and vegetables such as onions, garlic, carrots, squash and potatoes are peeled.
- We always bake with golden caster sugar and unsalted butter, unless otherwise indicated in the recipe, and test all recipes with semi-skimmed milk.

COOKING TIPS

- Recipes are tested in conventional ovens, using oven thermometers. For fan-assisted ovens, we advise reducing the oven temperature by 10–20C.
- We test if cakes are done by inserting a metal skewer into the centre. If the skewer comes out clean amd dry, the cake is cooked.
- When cooking chickens and turkeys, make sure they're cooked through. The safest way is to use a meat thermometer. Hold it for two minutes between the breast and thigh (the thickest part of the bird). A good-quality chicken or turkey needs to reach at least 70C; a cheaper one should reach 82C. If you don't have a thermometer, check the juices – they need to run clear when you pierce the thigh, and none of the meat should be pink.
- To sterilise a jar, wash the jar and lid (remove the rubber seal); place in the oven at 120C/gas ½ for 20 minutes, until dry. Immerse the seal in a pan of boiling water and simmer for 10 minutes; remove with tongs. If reusing jam jars, wash the jars and lids; heat in a low oven.
- We use mixing bowls made from non-reactive materials, such as glass, ceramic or plastic, to prevent acidic reactions from marinades.

NUTRITIONAL BREAKDOWN

Nutritional values may vary from those published here. Serving sizes are based on recipe recommendations and don't generally include extras - for example, "Crème fraîche, to serve". To see how we nutritionally analyse our recipes, and what we base our health claims on, please visit jamieoliver.com/nutritiondisclaimer.